Thanks be to God for his gift in Ella Williamson! *For Hurting Women in the Workplace* gives female marketplace ministers a timely and transparent word of encouragement to help advance the Kingdom of God in an unprecedented way; and a poignant reminder that we are God's emissaries at all times and in all places!

—Tasha Douglas, Author of *Sistershout!*

Ella Williamson's *Hurting Women in the Workplace: It's Time to Heal God's Way* is a thought-provoking book that delves deep beneath the surface of the roles many women play at work, exposing some of the psycho-emotional/spiritual torque at play in their work relationships. Well supported by scripture, *Hurting Women in the Workplace* points to the need for all employers, supervising staff, and supporting staff to take a more spirit-involved look at the little-talked-about dynamics in operation behind the scenes of, probably, most work environments. Written with much compassion and insight.

—Esther Davis-Thompson, *author of From Trouble to High Places: Meditations for Women Who Are So Ready to Cross the Bridges that Lead to Joy!*

Ella's book is a thought-provoking read for women of all ages and stages in search of healing and purpose in and out of the workplace.

—Doris Person, Ed.D.

For Hurting Women in the Workplace: It's Time to Heal God's Way is inspirational, realistic, resourceful, and insightful. It includes strategies based on biblical principles and scriptural guidance to assist in the healing process of hurting women in the workplace.

—Judy Gee-Moses, CCS, friend

Ella truly speaks from a heart that beats for God! She knows her purpose in life and wants to help reach those who are not aware of their own pain. Her words and those she shares from the Word of God helps direct those who need to know the way. May you find that comfort, encouragement, and healing that Ella so graciously shares.

—Debbie Swain, Christian businesswoman

For Hurting Women
in the Workplace

For Hurting Women in the Workplace

It's time to heal God's way

Ella M. Williamson

TATE PUBLISHING & Enterprises

Scripture quotations marked "KJV" are taken from the *Holy Bible, King James Version*, Cambridge, 1769. Used by permission. All rights reserved.

Scripture quotations marked "TAB" are taken from *The Amplified Bible, Old Testament*, Copyright © 1965, 1987 by the Zondervan Corporation and The Amplified New Testament, Copyright © 1958, 1987 by The Lockman Foundation. Used by permission. All rights reserved.

Scripture quotations are taken from *The Believer's Bible Commentary*, Copyright © 1985 by Thomas Nelson Publishers. Used by permission. All rights reserved.

Scripture quotations are taken from *NIV/KJV Parallel Bible*, Copyright © 1983 by International Bible Society. Used by permission. All rights reserved.

The opinions expressed by the author are not necessarily those of Tate Publishing, LLC.

Published by Tate Publishing & Enterprises, LLC
127 E. Trade Center Terrace | Mustang, Oklahoma 73064 USA
1.888.361.9473 | www.tatepublishing.com

Tate Publishing is committed to excellence in the publishing industry. The company reflects the philosophy established by the founders, based on Psalm 68:11,
"The Lord gave the word and great was the company of those who published it."

Book design copyright © 2009 by Tate Publishing, LLC. All rights reserved.
Cover design by Kellie Southerland
Interior design by Stephanie Woloszyn

Published in the United States of America

ISBN: 978-1-60799-667-5
1. Religion / Christian Life / Women's Issues
2. Religion / Christian Life / Professional Growth
09.06.25

The Journey

by Mary Oliver

One day you finally knew
what you had to do, and began,
though the voices around you
kept shouting
their bad advice—
though the whole house
began to tremble
and you felt the old tug
at your ankles.
"Mend my life!"
each voice cried.
But you didn't stop.
You knew what you had to do,
though the wind pried
with its stiff fingers
at the very foundations,
though their melancholy
was terrible.
It was already late
enough, and a wild night,
and the road full of fallen
branches and stones.

But little by little,
as you left their voices behind,
the stars began to burn
through the sheets of clouds,
and there was a new voice
that you slowly
recognized as your own,
that kept you company
as you strode deeper and deeper
into the world,
determined to do
the only thing you could do—
determined to save
the only life you could save.

Dedication

With love and gratitude, I dedicate this book to all our daughters … the working women of tomorrow.

The writing of this book has been accomplished as a result of friends, colleagues, and family members encouraging me every step of the way. To all those ladies who urged me to keep writing because they knew this book would heal so many women drifting on the sea of hurt experienced in the workplace, thank you. Thanks to all my women friends who shared with me the heartbreaks they've endured in the workplace. I have spent countless hours in front of the computer striving to accurately tell their stories and mine.

Writing a book is not easy, but God says, "Not by might, nor by power, but by the spirit" (Zechariah 4:6, KJV). This was definitely true on days when my carpal tunnel syndrome was causing much pain in my writing arm and hand. I cling to these holy words through my faith, believing that if God has commissioned any one of us to complete a task, he will not just help us get started and then leave us, but he will make provisions for us to complete it.

So I answered and spake to the angel that talked with me, saying, what are these, my LORD? Then the angel that talked with me answered and said unto me, knowest thou not what these be? And I said, No my Lord. Then he answered and spake unto me saying, This is the word of the Lord unto Zerubbabel, saying, Not by might, nor by power, but by my spirit, saith the Lord of hosts.

Zechariah 4:4–6, KJV

It is my hope that this book will lift the fog from the eyes of the loving women who are your birth mothers. I pray that they will see more clearly the need to rise higher in the workplace to show working women of tomorrow hope, not helplessness; to show power, not powerlessness; to show faith, not fear; to show success, not scars; to show love, not hate; to show competition, not deceit; and finally, to show how to be leaders, not followers.

As I was with Moses, so I will be with you; I will not fail you or forsake you. Be strong (confident) and of good courage, for you shall cause this people to inherit the land which I swore to their fathers to give them. Only you be strong and very courageous, that you may do according to all the law which Moses My servant commanded you. Turn not from it to the right hand or to the left, that you may prosper wherever you go. This Book of the Law shall not depart out of your mouth, but you shall mediate on it day and night, that you may observe and do according to all that is written in it. For then you shall make your way prosperous, and then you shall deal wisely and have good success. Have not I commanded you? Be strong, vigorous, and very courageous. Be not afraid, neither be dismayed, for the LORD your God is with you wherever you go.

Joshua 1:1–9, TAB

It is also my desire that young women who are the future workforce of tomorrow will learn that no one can nurture another human being if they are tired, burned out, and broken—spiritually and mentally bankrupt; however, through God's guidance, a new pattern can be forged in the workplace that leads these young women onto their path for passionate living, learning, dreaming, and doing. To these younger ones following in our footsteps, I want to say that I hope we will be the keepers of your dreams, the protectors of your joy, the singers of your unsung songs, and the restorers of your divine restoration. We are the light unto your path that will show you how to overcome hurt, frustration, and pain. But more importantly, it is our highest calling to introduce you to God's grace, love, and forgiveness.

Ye are the light of the world. A city that is set on a hill cannot be hid. Neither do men light a candle, and put it under a bushel, but on a candlestick; and it giveth light unto all that are in the house. Let your light so shine before men, that they may see your good works, and glorify your father which is in heaven.

Matthew 5:14–16, KJV

The Believer's Bible Commentary discusses how these verses imply that as disciples of Jesus Christ, our main function in the workplace is to be the salt of the earth. Jesus also calls us to be the light of the world, which includes our place of employment. "The Christian is like a city that is set on a hill in the workplace; it is elevated about its surroundings and it shines in the midst of darkness. Those whose lives exhibit the traits of Christ's teaching cannot be hidden."[1]

So, may the words in this book lift off these pages and elope into your heart to create a legacy that will teach you to focus on the Creator and not human creatures. When the Creator designed you, he made you as an original, and there will never be anyone like you on this earth ever again. By acknowledging the Creator, you accept all your mistakes without regrets, and you feel a sense of gratitude and glory when you overcome hurt in the workplace without suffering lingering or permanent scars. When you know that you are divinely created, you sing your own songs while keeping a balance between self and worldly possessions.

> By acknowledging the Creator, you accept all your mistakes without regrets, and you feel a sense of gratitude and glory when you overcome hurt in the workplace without suffering lingering or permanent scars.

Trust in the LORD with all thine heart; and lean not, unto thine own understanding. In all thy ways acknowledge him and he shall direct thy paths.

Proverbs 3:5–6, KJV

We have to acknowledge God in our workplace as the ultimate supervisor: "In all of your ways acknowledge him," simply means that every area of our lives must be turned over to God's control. "We must have no will of our own, only a single pure desire to know his will and to do it. If these conditions are met, the promise is that God shall direct our paths. He may do it through the Bible, through the advice of godly Christians, through the marvelous converging of circumstances, through the inward peace of the Spirit, or through a combination of these. But if we wait, he will make the guidance so clear that to refuse would be positive disobedience."[2]

Therefore, working women of tomorrow, remember that your strength in the workplace is not in your job title or social status, but in your self-realization, your self-appreciation, and your self-love.

Charm and grace are deceptive, and beauty is vain (because it is not lasting), but a woman who reverently and worshipfully fears the LORD, she shall be praised!

Proverbs 31:30, TAB

A Version of Psalm 23 for the Workplace

Author Unknown

The Lord is my real boss, and I shall not want.
He gives me peace when chaos is all around me.
He gently reminds me to pray and do all things without
murmuring and complaining.

He reminds me that He is my source and not my job.
He restores my sanity every day and
guides my decisions that
I might honor Him in all that I do.

Even though I face absurd amounts
of e-mails, system crashes,
unrealistic deadlines, budget cutbacks, gossiping co-workers,
discriminating supervisors and an aging body that doesn't
cooperate every morning, I still will not stop—for He is
with me! His presence, His peace, and
His power will see me through.

He raises me up, even when they fail to promote me.
He claims me as His own, even
when the company threatens

to let me go. His faithfulness and love
is better than any bonus check.

His retirement plan beats every 401k there is!
When it's all said and done,
I'll be working for Him a whole lot
longer and for that, I *bless His name!*

Acknowledgments

This book was born out of a labor of love. Patricia, Mamie, Parphine, Latile, Marshell, Chandler, Vanessa, Robert, Earlene, Angra, Letha, Cecila, Chandler F., Ashley, Dana, Renata, Asian, Shannon, Courtney, Jamar, Geordi, Arabia, Ricco, Tywon, Rahiem, Anthony, and Alexis—as my precious family members, you are both my inspiration and my salvation. You have been my compass during times of uncertainty in my personal life. Your love has provided me a place of normalcy and stability, and it has been my safe harbor whenever I've needed a place to dock.

My editors and supporters, Janet Angelo and Letha Brailsford, gave me encouragement as well as additional advice and friendship.

I thank God for blessing me with two wonderful parents, Chandler and Bessie Williamson, Sr., for without their guidance and teachings I would be nothing. You are the source of my success, and I love both of you more than life itself.

For all of you who were gracious enough to share your stories with me, please know how much you mean to me. Although your name is not mentioned here, always know that you have not gone unacknowledged in my heart. This entire book could be filled with your names alone, so please know I thank all of you who have not been named individually, but you know who you are.

And most importantly, to my Lord and Savior Jesus Christ, I want to say thank you for giving me courage to believe in myself when others doubted. Thank you for letting me realize that I can do all things through Jesus Christ who strengthens me. Thank you for teaching me how to let go of the past and press toward the mark of the high calling.

Contents

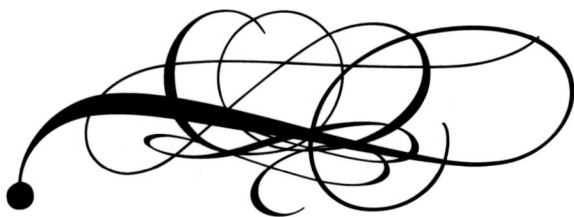

Preface

Therefore, if any person is (ingrafted) in Christ (the Messiah) he is a new creation (a new creature altogether); the old (previous moral and spiritual condition) has passed away. Behold, the fresh and new has come!

2 Corinthians 5:17, TAB

You may be wondering why I selected women, versus men, to discuss in this book. As we all know, men and women are totally different creatures when it comes to expressing emotions and thoughts, and being a woman, I knew that I could inherently relate to the subject matter as it affects women. Also, I think it is more common for women to turn to the workplace setting as a temporary escape from abusive relationships, financial problems, parental burnout, the stress of dealing with childcare issues, and from feeling overwhelmed with depressing thoughts, loneliness, and isolation.

Men deal with failure and emotional difficulties by using logical reasoning, but women deal with failure and pain through their emotions, which often results in misplaced anger. In other words, they seek to place the blame upon another person who frequently has nothing to do with the offense. Men normally come to work to simply get the job done, but women frequently use the workplace as a way to escape unresolved issues in their lives. Men absorb their displeasure at work internally, whereas women verbally expose their displeasure by making comments like "I'm having a bad day" or "I'm going to find another job." In my observation, when men are faced with a problem in the workplace, they address it with the appropriate staff person to work toward a solution. They do not run around the office looking for sympathy from others.

The workplace is a fertile ground for Satan to pull his tricks, simply because there are so many women available for him to deceive who are seeking validation from other people around them instead of from God. Satan does not want God to be pleased with our behavior in the workplace. Don't forget, Satan's biggest gripe is with God. Our enemy's chief goal is to get revenge back at God for not putting up with his secret wishes to be like the Supreme Being. Satan is already defeated by God, so he does everything he can to disturb God's heart by targeting his believers. The enemy seeks to bring separation and division between employers and employees, as well as between believers, churches of different denominations (or even the same), friends, and between parents and children and husbands and wives. Satan's attacks are often psychological or in our emotions, and he does not use logical reasoning. Therefore, as women in the workplace who operate primarily from an emotional standpoint, we often look at situations as being unfair or someone else's fault, or we turn our attacks inward and think, *I am stupid; I will never be able to conquer this problem.*

In my opinion, many hurting women seek a job outside the home for socialization, to make friends, to plan after work "beat down the supervisor" parties, to discuss male issues, to complain about childcare issues, and to meet potential mates. In my observation as an administrator over the past fifteen years, I've noticed that many hurting women bring *home* to *work* and then *work* to *home*, a cycle that leads to constant turmoil and confusion for them personally, and for their families.

Grumbling among just a few women in the workplace can lead to a deluge of women giving out false reports or spreading unnecessary rumors. Grumbling is a bad preoccupation. It makes you look backward, like Lot's wife, who turned into a pillar of salt. An unseen barrier can emerge between you and God when you are looking back and grumbling about the past. Instead of grumbling, we should take our complaints straight to God. However, if we are going to move into our place of promise in him, we must shed negative conversations and grumbling altogether and start living our lives with unwavering faithfulness.

> Grumbling among just a few women in the workplace can lead to a deluge of women giving out false reports or spreading unnecessary rumors.

But the human tongue can be tamed by no man. It is a restless (undisciplined, irreconcilable) evil, full of deadly poison. With it we curse men who were made in God's likeness! Out of the same mouth come forth blessing and cursing. These things, my brethren, ought not to be so.

James 3:8–10, TAB

To be a sincere person in the workplace we must not bless and curse out of our mouths at the same time. If we really want to make an impact in the business world, we must demonstrate that we truly have repented by manifesting a transformed life. Genuine repentance produces fruits.[3]

The biggest issue facing most hurting women in the workplace is insecurity. Insecurity means "lacking emotional stability; not well-adjusted. Lacking self-confidence; plagued by anxiety."[4]

When a woman is insecure and has unresolved emotional and psychological issues, this inner turmoil often gets acted out in a variety of ways in the workplace, such as being consistently late for work, seeking attention from superiors by being non-compliant with job duties, gossiping with co-workers, soliciting co-workers to help sabotage team-building efforts, inappropriate relationships with clients, manipulation of male bosses, always being the first to arrive at the office to stake out control for the day, being the last to leave the office to create the persona of being a committed worker (when in reality she doesn't want to face her life after work), and so on.

Most hurting women are still searching for their place and purpose in the world, even though they may have a college education and many years of work experience. Hurting women come from all walks of life—from all races and nationalities and from many different religious affiliations. Hurting women are young, old, withdrawn, disoriented, unpredictable, and "sick and tired of being sick and tired." They experience depression, fear, low self-esteem, doubt, bitterness, and self-pity. I have known hurting women of all ages, but it is especially disheartening to see older hurting women in the workplace, because often the younger women are searching for role models and mentors to help them excel and achieve great things. Many older women never want to reveal to the younger women what they have done wrong, the mistakes they have made, the hurt and pain they have felt, the relationships they have had outside of marriage, and the babies they may have had out of wedlock. This is a shame, because sharing their own painful experiences and mistakes could help steer the younger women from doing the same.

The common denominator among hurting women is that they are lost when it comes to knowing their purpose and meaning for living. They just exist with a job title, feeling powerless to explore their abilities or to know their true, God-given purpose and destiny. Authority means "power to influence or persuade resulting from knowledge or experience; confidence derived from experience or practice; firm self-assurance."[5]

I had to be healed God's way from the many emotional wounds that were inflicted upon me in the workplace. God showed me how he had used every circumstance I faced in my workplace to create an opportunity for me to praise him in the midst of terrible adversity. Adversity means "a state of hardship or affliction; misfortune."[6]

Now he has called me to share my healing with others, as well as given me the opportunity to do so. If you are a woman who has been hurt in the workplace, I want you to know that you can trust others again, because tomorrow is always a new day when the sun will once again rise in the east. Malachi 4:2–3 (TAB) reinforces this statement when it says, "But unto you that revere and worshipfully fear My name shall the Sun of Righteousness arise with healing in His wings. You shall tread down the wicked; for they shall be ashes under the soles of your feet in the day that I shall do this, saith the Lord of hosts."

In other words, "We should not lose heart and grow weary and faint in acting nobly and doing right, for in due time and at the appointed season we shall reap, if we do not loosen and relax our courage and faint" (Galatians 6:9, TAB). As it states in the *Believer's Bible Commentary*, "Lest any should become discouraged, Paul reminds his readers that the rewards are certain, even if not immediate. You do not harvest a field of wheat the day after you sow the seed. So in the spiritual realm, the rewards surely follow faithful sowing in due season."[7]

However, in order for you to claim this scripture for your life, you have to make sure that you are not one of those women trying to hurt other women in the workplace; women who are also trying to find their path in this journey called life. Your true fulfillment lies in finding your identity in Christ Jesus.

> And I will give you the treasures of darkness and hidden riches of secret places, that you may know that it is I, the Lord, the God of Israel, who calls you by your name.
>
> Isaiah 45:3, TAB

Many women are hurting because they measure their worth against worldly possessions and frivolous things. They believe they will be happy simply by having a certain job title in the secular world. Hurting women bounce back and forth between jobs, co-workers, friends, relationships, and even churches, trying to find answers to their life's problems. In order to resolve their identity crisis, however, they must first be identified with Christ Jesus.

> But seek ye first the kingdom of God, and his righteousness; and all these things shall be added unto you as well.
>
> Matthew 6:33, KJV

Here, God makes a covenant with believers, that if we put his interests first in our lives, he will guarantee our future needs. If we seek first the kingdom of God and his righteousness, then he will see to it that we never lack the necessities of life.[8]

So many people go to work every day and to church on the weekend, but they hate their lives and lack the basic necessities of life. Having the right job but with a worried mind and a wrong attitude will never equal success. On the contrary, having the right inspiration given by the divine Creator who made heaven and earth will create a masterpiece flowered with motivation, success, internal healing, and a professionally developed landscape in the goodness of God.

> On the contrary, having the right inspiration given by the divine Creator who made heaven and earth will create a masterpiece flowered with motivation, success, internal healing, and a professionally developed landscape in the goodness of God.

I hope this book helps hurting women in the workplace, in the church pews, and all over the world. I hope the information found in this text will mend the broken hearts of women who have been wounded in the workplace, and that it will offer strategies on how to survive in the workplace with women who may be determined to hurt others because of their own insecurities and pain.

The LORD our God spake unto us in Horeb, saying, Ye have dwelt long enough in this mount.

Deuteronomy 1:6, KJV

Paradoxical Commandments of Leadership

Author Unknown

People are illogical, unreasonable, and self-centered; love them anyway.

If you do good, people will accuse you of selfish, ulterior motives; do good anyway.

If you are successful, you will win false friends and true enemies; succeed anyway.

The good you do today will perhaps be forgotten tomorrow; do good anyway.

Honesty and frankness may make you vulnerable; be honest and frank anyway.

The biggest man with the biggest ideas can be shot down by the smallest man with the smallest mind; think big anyway.

People favor underdogs but follow only hot dogs; fight for the few underdogs anyway.

What you spend years building may be destroyed overnight; build anyway.

People really need help but may attack you if you help them; help them anyway.

Give the world the best that you have and you will get kicked in the teeth; give the world the best that you have anyway.

If better is possible, then good is not good enough.

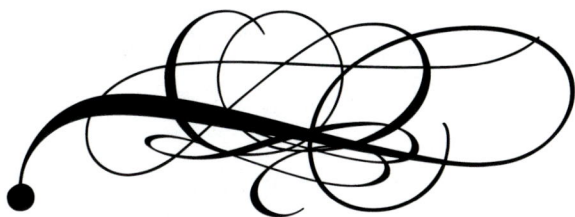

Chapter 1

Overcoming Hurt in the Workplace God's Way

Karen was a successful businesswoman, working her way up the corporate ladder God's way. She had become friends with several women who worked in her office. Karen, not knowing that many of her women friends had yet to be liberated (breaking free from mental and emotional disabilities to enter into their promise land) from Satan's avalanche of unconfessed sin, would experience very bad treatment. Until God opened her eyes like he did the blind man at the pool, she endured countless acts of cruelty because secretly her women friends desired to be advanced in the company. Many of Karen's women friends reported untruths to her boss and covertly attempted to get her fired from her position.

After more than a decade of dealing with bankrupt women, Karen finally had a light bulb go off in her head that hurting people hurt others. Karen was able to realize that her mishaps in the workplace were God ordained to help her walk down the road to Calvary (there is no resurrection without a crucifixion). Karen now knows that if she had not suffered in the workplace, she would not have developed her radical dependence on God for his leadership in the workplace. Karen sees the beauty inside her disappointments and all she has gained after losing so much.

What a lot of women did not know about Karen was that she was a hurting woman until she met someone who ministered to her through the Word of God. Although Karen was a successful business-woman, she had to overcome several hurdles that pierced her in the side until the pain flowed free, just like Jesus' blood and water ran at the Cross of Calvary. Karen is biologically connected to Jesus Christ, and she knows that she doesn't need a birth certificate to show that she belongs to the Kingdom of God. Karen knows her biological con-nection to Jesus Christ makes her famous, so she doesn't seek notori-ety in the workplace by hurting others.

Karen knows that when you are at your all-time low in the workplace, God is up to something in your life. The distraction by ungodly and godly folks in the workplace is to keep a person from seeing their deliverance that is just around the corner. God sees when righteous men and women try to lock us away from his embrace with their worldly judgment. Karen knows that nothing can separate her from the love of God, no matter what weapon is formed against her in the workplace.

He said: listen, King Jehoshaphat and all who live in Judah and Jerusalem! This is what the LORD says to you: Do not be afraid or discouraged because of this vast army. For the battle is not yours, but God's. Tomorrow march down against them. They will be climbing up by the Pass of Ziz, and you will find them at the end of the gorge in the Desert of Jeruel. You will not have to fight this battle. Take up your positions; stand firm and see the deliverance the LORD will give

you, O Judah and Jerusalem. Do not be afraid; do
not be discouraged. Go out to face them tomorrow, and the LORD will be with you.

> 2 Chronicles 20:15–17, NIV

As a woman, some of the most heart-wrenching things
I've endured have happened to me in the workplace. As
you may guess, most of this bad treatment was delivered
by the hands of women whom I had tried to nurture,
mature, support, and help move up the ladder of success.
I will cover this in more detail later in the book, but the
point I want to make here at the outset is that sometimes we are selected to suffer for God's glory. Satan may
attempt to upset us, but he can never defeat us because
the head of the serpent has already been crushed by the
heel of Jesus.

I was always taught that as a successful African-
American female I should reach out and help others
as well. Buying into this "give back" motto, I hired and
mentored several women and gave them opportunities
to advance in the workplace. Although my loyalty and
commitment to them was not always reciprocated, I still
believe we must serve others just as Christ gave his life
for a ransom for all of our sins and shortcomings.

> For one is regarded favorably (is approved,
> acceptable, and thank-worthy) if, as in the sight
> of God, he endures the pain of unjust suffering.
> (After all) what kind of glory (is there in it) if,
> when you do wrong and are punished for it, you
> take it patiently? But if you bear patiently with

suffering (which results) when you do right and that is undeserved, it is acceptable and pleasing to God.

1 Peter 2:19–20, TAB

When we suffer unjustly in the workplace, we win God's approval. He is pleased when he finds us so conscious of our relation to him that we endure underserved pain without vindicating self or fighting back. When we meekly take unjust treatment, we display Christ; this supernatural life gains God's "well done." There is no virtue in patient suffering for our own misdeeds. Certainly there is no glory for God in it. Such suffering will never mark us out as Christians, or make others want to become Christians. But suffering patiently for well-doing is the thing that counts. It is so unnatural, so other worldly that it shocks people into conviction of sin and, hopefully, into salvation.[9]

After taking the knives out of my back, I evaluated what I had done to drive some of these women to execute such vengeful, backstabbing, and sabotaging behavior toward me. However, in conducting a true assessment of my own behavior, thoughts, and attitude, and after much soul searching, I realized that most of these women had severe emotional issues, which they had shared with me in confidence (as their supervisor) during weekly review meetings. Many of my female employees would thank me for helping them or say something like, "Ms. Williamson, I hope to reach your level of success one day." I thought these were genuine comments, but in reality they were warning signs of things to come. I have since discovered that comments like these are often a hurting woman's cry for help, because in essence she is saying, "I hate my life and wish it could be like yours."

I needed to write this book for me. These written words caused me to search my soul, and thus they became the symbol that best expressed what I had encountered in the workplace. The words in this book, along with the experiences I endured with these hurting women, ordered my life into a process that completed my identity.

> Consider it wholly joyful, my brethren, whenever you are enveloped in or encounter trials of any sort or fall into various temptations. Be assured and understand that the trial and proving of your faith bring out endurance and steadfastness and patience. But let endurance and steadfastness and patience have full play and do a thorough work, so that you may be (people) perfectly and fully developed (with no defects), lacking in nothing.
>
> James 1:2–4, TAB

In these verses James deals with the subject of temptation. The Christian life is filled with problems. They come uninvited and unexpected. Sometimes they come singly and sometimes in droves. They are inevitable. "But let patience have its perfect work," says James. Sometimes when we're deluged with problems we become desperate and use whatever frantic means we think are necessary to cut short the trial. Without consulting the Lord as to his purposes in the matter, we do whatever we can to shorten the trial. By doing this we actually may be thwarting God's program in our lives. And because we have cut short what he was trying to teach us, it is also possible that we may have to undergo a longer trial in the future before his particular purpose is realized in us. We should not short-circuit the development of endurance in our lives. By cooperating with God we will become mature, well-rounded Christians, lacking in none of the graces of the Spirit.[10]

When I became the brunt of unsolicited, cruel behavior that was directed at me from hurting women in the workplace, it taught me how to accept rejection just like our Savior, Jesus Christ, endured. According to scripture, Jesus was rejected by his own nation. God accepted this rejection without dipping into a state of depression or despair.

> Jesus asked them, Have you never read in the Scriptures; The very Stone which the builders rejected and threw away has become the Cornerstone; this is the LORD's doing, and it is marvelous in our eyes?
>
> Matthew 21:42, TAB

When Christ, the Stone, presented himself to the builders—the leaders of Israel, they had no place for him in their building plans. They threw him aside as useless. But following his death he was raised from the dead and given the place of preeminence by God. He has been made the topmost stone in God's building: God also has highly exalted him and given him the name which is above every name.[11]

Working in a hostile and resentful work environment can cause a woman's mind to doubt her abilities and diminish the impact her talents and gifts have had on her company's success. This sort of negative environment can also limit her possibilities and dilute the dreams she has for herself.

Thankfully, by God's grace I never allowed the rejection to alter my attitude and behavior. I never stopped believing that my life and work were predestined by God, and that no matter what happened, no one could stop me from carrying out his purpose for my life while I reside in this earthly body.

> Behold! I have given you authority and power to trample upon serpents and scorpions, and (physical and mental strength and ability) over all the power that the enemy (possesses): and nothing shall in any way harm you.
>
> Luke 10:19, TAB

The Lord gave his disciples authority against the forces of evil, and likewise he has given us authority in the workplace. The disciples were granted immunity from harm during their mission, and this is true of all God's servants—we are protected.[12]

God delivered me from depression, anxiety, confusion, sleepless nights, and brokenness. He helped me to work through and dissolve my pain so that he could recycle it into something good. God created the world's existence from nothing, and he can take the crumbled ruins of your life and create them into a mosaic of good things. What God created in you was good, and you were born to glorify him.

> Even every one that is called by my name: for I have created him for my glory, I have formed him; yea, I have made him.
>
> Isaiah 43:7, KJV

If we can endure the afflictions thrust upon us by our trusted women friends, then certainly we can survive the disappointments that life will hurl at us. A season of hurting is a small price to pay for a continuous harvest of blessings born out of your surrendering to God's guidance and direction for your life. Faith is not gained from brownie points earned serving on church committees, or from being the most "religious," but only through climbing out of the valley, up the mountain, and into Jesus' loving arms. A storm in your life often serves as a bulldozer uprooting the rubble from your mind to make the landscape of your heart clearer.

A storm in your life often serves as a bulldozer uprooting the rubble from your mind to make the landscape of your heart clearer.

I want to stop here and share my personal story and the hardship I suffered in my younger years, because often-times when we look at successful people we don't know the price they paid to attain their current position. A person's job title and lengthy résumé do not reveal their truth sense of self. It is only through knowing someone's personal history that you can really understand how they arrived at a particular assignment preordained for them by God. Therefore, the making of this book was set in time long before I took my first breath as a baby girl on August 17, 1963. My life was being shaped by adversity (and thus the contents of this book) long before I penned these words.

Humble Beginnings

I was born and raised in a quiet little town called Coward, South Carolina, which is located in Florence County. The population is around 650 based on the 2000 census. Coward is about seventy-three miles east of Columbia, South Carolina, and 106 miles southeast of Charlotte, North Carolina. It is part of the Florence Metropolitan Statistical Area. In doing my research for this book, I learned that Coward was settled by William McGee in the 1770s; he had cleared the land for his log cabin and thus could claim it. Originally the settlement was called Lynch. The name was later changed to Coward in honor of Asbury Coward, a native son who became commander of the Citadel Military College in Charleston, South Carolina.

For they all threw in out of their abundance; but she, out of her deep poverty, has put in everything that she had (even) all she had on which to live.

Mark 12:44, TAB

My first job at the age of twelve was working in a tobacco field. My uncle, Clennel Williamson, was my first boss, coach, and mentor. He would always tell me that I was going to be successful in the world because I was a steady and hard worker, even at the tender age of twelve. Uncle Clennel promoted me to work out in the field instead of just at the tobacco barn. Working at the tobacco barn was considered easy because the workers were just responsible for taking the tobacco off the drag and putting it into the barn to be cured. The work in the fields was a lot harder and much more tedious. Being promoted to the tobacco fields with the other workers meant I had to get accustomed to all kinds of insects, wet tobacco plants (especially in the morning hours), and long hours in the hot sun. However, I was proud of myself because Uncle Clennel told me I would someday be someone great and special because of my work ethic.

My parents are Bessie and Chandler Williamson, and both their roots are richly tied to the South. My father was a sharecropper and then a steelworker for Soccer Steel for more than twenty years. My father served in World War II. I have two wonderful parents who did not have a lot of financial means. My parents had twelve children, and I am the ninth child of this gang. Although we did not have a lot of financial resources, we did get a big dosage of the importance of education and being a respectful person. I came to appreciate this more as an adult. Sometimes looking back I thought my life was not good, especially after meeting other people in college and discovering how poor we really were. Over the years I missed out on a lot of opportunities to be in clubs and other activities because my parents could not afford it. However, I also realized how really blessed I was that my parents had taught us to work for whatever we got in life and to not put such a high value on material things.

Although my mother only completed the tenth grade and my father the sixth grade, they both made sure we got an education. They helped me to see education as the way out of poverty. I was the first person in my family to receive a Master's Degree on a full academic scholarship from the Ohio State University. (I should mention that all twelve of my parents' children received some type of continuing education training and/or a college degree, and we are all working in respectable jobs and doing the right things in life.)

Paternal History

My father's parents were Douglas Avon Williamson and Pearl Hall Williamson. Douglas was born in Coward, South Carolina, on April 18, 1895, and Grandma Pearl was born on May 8, 1903. They were married on August 20, 1919, and from their union thirteen children were born. Grandma Pearl's deepest desire for all her children was that they accept Jesus as their Lord and Savior. As a spiritual woman, she counseled the other women in the community. She was known as a woman who could keep secrets. She was also known to share her blessings with others in her family and community. Grandma Pearl loved serving God in her church by displaying the presence of the Holy Spirit in her shouts. She had a beautiful soprano voice and sang in the senior choir. Her favorite hymn was "Jesus Keep Me Near the Cross."

Grandma Pearl was a dedicated mother who was known to pray out loud. She would often pray while washing the dishes and would throw her dishcloth for emphasis. She made fervent supplication to the Lord in her home. She had two sons, Ocie and Chandler, both of whom went overseas to fight in World War II. She prayed diligently for their safe return. After returning home from the war, her son Chandler (my father) told her about a day (while in the combat zone) when his commanding officer kept him from going to a particular battle site with the rest of his platoon. That day his entire platoon was killed. Pearl asked him what day this happened. He told her and she responded, "Thank You, Jesus! That was the day I was in deep prayer for you."

Grandma Pearl was a woman who believed in prayer. A few days before she became sick and passed away, she attended the prayer meeting at her church. She testified that "everything looked white and her soul was pure." She left this world and entered into eternal glory on Friday, September 16, 1949.

Although I never got a chance to know or meet Grandma Pearl, through oral history and stories about her I know she weathered a lot of things through her faith.

I did know my grandpa Douglas. He departed this

life on Saturday, August 8, 1987, at the age of ninety-two. According to family history, Grandpa Douglas walked three miles to be educated in small classrooms held in the church. He was baptized around the age of sixteen in the Lynches River. As a youth he played baseball, fished, and listened to a wind-up phonograph for entertainment. His parents were fortunate enough to buy an organ that cost $85.00. They paid for it on an installment plan. Grandpa Douglas bought a piano book and taught himself how to play. He spent many hours each day practicing the organ. Grandpa Douglas sang and played with the church choir. He later became chairman of the senior choir.

Grandpa Douglas farmed tobacco, cotton, and corn as his commercial crops, and of course he grew vegetables to provide for his own family. Grandpa Douglas was also a shoe repairman and a barber. At one time he owned his own barbershop and charged a quarter a haircut. Grandpa Douglas was fortunate enough to purchase a Model T Ford.

Grandpa Douglas was a praying man. He loved to sing. He knew a number of hymns by memory. At the end of his long life, he prayed that the Lord would take him home. He had always felt that he was a stranger in this world, and he longed to be with the Lord.

Maternal History

My mother, Bessie Williamson, was a housewife. She kept all of us in line and worked hard to ensure that we knew right from wrong. My mother was born to Mamie Catherine Graham and Lewis Graham.

My grandmother Mamie Graham loved honey graham cookies and ice cream. I remember so affectionately how she would send us to the corner store in the late afternoon to get her some honey graham cookies and ice cream. Often she would baby-sit us when my parents went out of town, and when we grew older we had to go over to her home to help work her farm.

Grandmother Mamie Graham was one of eight children born to Johnny Edwards and Mary Jane Rush. Their parents (my great grandparents) were born to Abner and Amy Rush, and we are not certain how their paths chanced to cross, but they did cross and the rest is history.

Great-Great-Grandfather Abner Rush is thought to have been born on or around November 21, 1844, and died May 30, 1904, at the age of fifty-nine. Great-Great-Grandmother Amy Johnson-Rush has been given the birth date of January 1, 1834. She died January 11, 1934, at the age of one hundred. They are buried in the Rush Cemetery on Friendfield Road adjacent to Mt. Rona Baptist Church in Effingham, South Carolina. They were born during the institution of slavery, and they were united in holy matrimony in 1866, one year after the Civil War ended. Legend has it that Amy was a beautiful woman with dark skin and lovely dark hair. It is said that she would wash it in a nearby river. Amy was also described as being short in stature but strikingly beautiful. Not much mention was given to the physical features of Abner Rush, except that he was a devout Christian and a fanatic about education. These values of Christianity and education were instilled in his children, grandchildren, and great-grandchildren, and will continue to be for generations to come.

Both Abner and Amy, as fate would have it, were

slaves in the Florence County, South Carolina, area. Undocumented information has it that when Abner became a "free man," he was given a few acres and five dollars. Josephine Rush-Timmons (grandmother Josephine) related that the first land he purchased was lost because of some legal technicalities that he did not fully understand. Even so, he did not despair; he continued to scrimp and save pennies. He worked hard and was finally able to purchase a tract of land that became known as Rushtown. This land is located along Rushtown Road in Effingham, South Carolina.

Great-Great-Grandpa Abner Rush knew how the Lord had blessed him and his family, and he was indeed thankful. He, along with others, wanted to start a place of worship. With the help of J. L. Smith, a white minister, they started a "bush shelter." Abner was one of the first deacons. Both Amy and Abner were dedicated church workers. Close by the bush shelter, which later became Mt. Rona Baptist Church, was the Rushes' cemetery. The cemetery's name was changed from Rush's Cemetery to Mt. Rona Church Cemetery in 1927. The Rush family believed in the "old-time religion" and held high moral standards for themselves and their children.

With the church in place, Abner and Amy began to focus on their children's education. They had no formal education themselves, but they wanted to build a school for their children. With this in mind, they donated the land on which the Rush School was to be built. This school enabled the Rush children and other children in the community to learn reading, writing, and arithmetic (the standard curriculum for a grammar school at the time). The older Rush children were sent to the city of Florence to further their education.

The life that I have is the result of a lot of hard work on my part and sacrifice on the part of my ancestors, who endured much so that their descendants could have a better future. My blessings are connected to my humble beginnings. God is outside of motivation and self-help books, but he most definitely dwells inside inspirational thoughts, dreams, and visions.

After enduring several painful encounters with those vicious women in my workplace, I tried to counsel and supervise them with coaching and mentoring. As I did this, I realized how deep-rooted pain can cause someone to want to inflict pain on another person or even harm them. Some of these hurting women would try to measure their self-worth by telling themselves that my circumstances were not as bad as their circumstances. We have all heard the old saying that "misery loves company." The problem with a lot of women in the workplace is that their eyes are fixed on someone else's dream, vision, and destiny. They desire so much to walk in someone else's shadow that they cannot see God's plan and purpose for their own lives. It is fine to have a mentor or a role model to look up to, but your road map through life should be the Word of God.

Most hurting women suffer needlessly in the workplace because they are wishing upon someone else's star as a way to gain their own stardom. They wander through life wishing they were more beautiful, wishing they had a bigger house, wishing they had a bigger car, wishing they had more money, wishing they were more outspoken, wishing they were less emotional, wishing they could wish their pain away, wishing they were happier, and wishing to be connected to the right people.

> Most hurting women suffer needlessly in the workplace because they are wishing upon someone else's star as a way to gain their own stardom.

What they don't wish for is how to tap into the rich values about themselves from inside their own internal buried treasures. Often when we want to model our lives after someone else's, we have no idea what sort of struggles they've endured or how their internal motives differ from ours. We don't know the situations they've been through in the past or what they might be coping with in the present. Most of all, we don't know what resides within their hearts.

> The steps of a good man are ordered by the LORD: and he delighteth in his way. Though he fall, he shall not be utterly cast down: for the LORD upholdeth him with his hand. I have been young, and now am old; yet have I not seen the righteous forsaken, not his seed begging bread. He is ever merciful, and lendeth; and his seed is blessed. Depart from evil, and do good; and dwell for evermore. For the LORD loveth judgment, and forsaketh not his saints; they are pre-

served forever: but the seed of the wicked shall be cut off. The righteous shall inherit the land, and dwell therein for ever. The mouth of the righteous speaketh wisdom, and his tongue talketh of judgment. The law of his God is in his heart; none of his steps shall slide.

Psalm 37:23–31, KJV

I think the other reason why I may have been viciously attacked is because I always remained silent about my personal life in the workplace, and I have the ability to live in my loneliness and yet still not be alone. Someone once told me, "Your silence speaks as loud as your actions." So many women in the workplace fill their lives up with people who mean them no good. They want to engage in conversation that destroys instead of edifies. Their conversations literally litter the workplace with empty words.

So let us then definitely aim for and eagerly pursue what makes for harmony and for mutual upbuilding (edification and development) of one another.

Romans 14:19, TAB

Instead of bickering over inconsequential matters, we should make every effort to maintain peace and harmony in Christian fellowship. Instead of causing others to stumble while we insist on our rights, we should strive to build them up in their most holy faith.[13]

Learning to live with silence and solitude has often been viewed by others as having a boring life or no life at all. However, until a person can entertain herself with her own thoughts and dreams, she will never know true serenity. Learning to live with yourself is about letting the anointing of the Holy Spirit rest on you until your thoughts are pure; your mind is right, your flesh is no longer weak and lusting for worldly things, your dreams and visions are coming to pass, and your fears have been replaced with faith. It's about finding a peace within that passes all understanding for those whose minds are stayed on Jesus Christ.

Many times I had to remain silent in the workplace just as Jesus did when he stood before his accusers in Pilate's court. "And the high priest stood up and said, 'Have you no answer to make? What about this that these men testify against you?' But Jesus kept silent" (Matthew 26:62–63). Following Jesus' example, there are times when we must steal away to our secret island and retreat into the arms of Jesus and meditate on our rejection and not respond; because the enemy does not know what to do if we remain silent. By being silent we do not carry around other people's stuff needlessly. The Bible says there is "a time to keep silence and a time to speak" (Ecclesiastes 3:7). In addition, the Bible teaches in Hebrews 12:15 that we should "watch out lest any root of bitterness springing up trouble you, and thereby many be defiled" (KJV).

Jesus was crucified; but prior to his crucifixion he was mocked, and his life's work was put on public display for all to judge. The same thing happens to us; sometimes our personal pain is publicly displayed, but when that happens, we can be encouraged because without a crucifixion, you can never have a resurrection.

Some of Jesus' critics should have been a witness of his goodness, but instead his friends (and some of his disciples) ran away from him and cried out, "Crucify him!" along with the rest of the crowd.

> So then Pilate took Jesus and scourged (flogged, whipped) Him. And the soldiers, having twisted together a crown of thorns, put it on His head, and threw a purple cloak around Him. And they kept coming to Him and saying, Hail, King of the Jews! (Good health to you! Peace to you! Long life to you, King of the Jews!) And they struck him with the palms of their hands. Then Pilate went out again and said to them, see, I bring him out to you, so that you may know that I find no fault (crime, cause for accusation) in Him.
>
> John 19:1–4, TAB

It was unjust for Pilate to scourge an innocent man. Perhaps he hoped the punishment would satisfy the Jews and they would not demand the death of Jesus, thus absolving him from having to pronounce such a heavy sentence. Scourging was a Roman form of punishment. The prisoner was beaten with a whip or a rod. The whip had pieces of metal or bone tied into the split ends of it, and these cut deep gashes into the flesh. The soldiers mocked Jesus' claim to be king, and to emphasize their mockery they made him a crown of thorns. This would have caused extreme pain as it was pressed onto his brow. Thorns are a symbol of the curse that sin brought to mankind, but the Lord Jesus bore the curse of our sins so that we might wear a crown of glory. The purple robe was also used in mockery. Purple was the color of royalty, but it reminds us of how our sins were placed on Jesus in order that we might be clothed with the robe of God's righteousness.[14]

When we are rejected, despised, abandoned, betrayed, shamed, and wounded by those who should love us or at least respect us, Jesus knows what it feels like. He offers us the greatest example of how to overcome hurt and rejection. The main difference between hurting women and non-hurting women is that non-hurting women have surrendered their healing to the Healer of the universe, and the heavenly surgeon has removed all "cancerous hurt cells" from the body.

This may sound surreal to some of you, but that's because it can only be comprehended in the supernatural realm. That's why it's good to have a lot of time alone—because it causes you to get clear instructions from God. Your alone time can lift you out of a deep hole and into victorious living, as well as become your companion and motivator to help manifest miracles in your life.

When I suffered mistreatment in the workplace, I learned some things about my heart—that I had the capacity to love and to show mercy but also to release anger and envy that can sometimes stay hidden until awakened by painful circumstances. I have learned that job satisfaction only comes from knowing that your job is a part of your assignment on this earth given to you by God. Therefore, we must walk and work joyously in the workplace setting while God reveals what we can ultimately provide for our employer in contrast to what our employer can provide for us.

The good news is that God took all of my hurt and turned it around in my life for my good and his glory. Through all the rejection, betrayal, and wrongful accusations thrust against me in my fifteen years in corporate America, I am able to say to all who hurt me, "You meant evil against me, but God meant it for good" (Genesis 50:20, NKJV).

He has commissioned me to minister to hurting people and to become a source of encouragement for people whose behavior in the workplace will never be improved until they draw closer to God. I knew pain and rejection, but I was able to overcome my dilemma not by focusing on trying to change my past, but by trusting God to change my present circumstances and future outcomes.

I find myself being favored by God because of my rejection; just like Mary was. She was rejected for being pregnant without a husband, but God selected her because he knew she could withstand the pressure.

> And he came to her and said, Hail, O favored one (endued with grace)! The LORD is with you! Blessed (favored of God) are you before all other women!
>
> Luke 1:28, TAB

The angel addressed Mary as one who was highly favored, one whom the Lord was visiting with special privilege, but the angel did not worship Mary or pray to her; he simply greeted her. He did not say that she was "full of grace," but that she was highly favored.[15]

T. D. Jake, in his book *Naked and Not Ashamed,* states, "One of the greatest challenges of our walk with God is to resist the temptation to allow what happened in the past to determine who we are today. We each must begin to understand and declare: 'I am not what happened yesterday. I endured what happened. I survived what happened, but I am not what happened yesterday!'"

Overcoming pain in the workplace and in any other stale places in our lives will happen only once we've surrendered our will to God. In addition, we have to accept responsibility that some of the personal pain and suffering we are experiencing is a result of choices we've made. When we accept these two things and offer no excuses or blame, God reveals his plan for our lives. He called us even while we were in our mother's womb, and his plan for us is that we prosper and be in good health.

When you have been truly set free from pain in the workplace, you will no longer allow others to damage your emotions with their unsolicited opinions that they feel they have a right to express about you.

Once a woman gets through the initial pain and betrayal in the workplace, she can then find avenues to grow as well as learn how to flow with the constant roller-coaster issues that crop up in the "newsroom cubicles" (gossip factories) of the workplace. If you are in just such an office environment, you can come to your workplace prepared to deal with the attacks *if* you are spending quality time every day with God studying his Word, praying, and fasting.

> Once a woman gets through the initial pain and betrayal in the workplace, she can then find avenues to grow as well as learn how to flow with the constant roller-coaster issues that crop up in the "newsroom cubicles" (gossip factories) of the workplace.

> He was guilty of no sin, neither was deceit (guile) ever found on His lips. When he was reviled and insulted, He did not revile or offer insult in return; He was abused and suffered, He made no threats (of vengeance); but he trusted (Himself and everything) to him Who judges fairly
>
> 1 Peter 2:22–23, TAB

Jesus did not suffer for his own sins because he had none. His speech was never tainted by deceit. He never lied or even shaded the truth. Think about that! A person once lived on this planet who was absolutely honest and absolutely free from trickery or deceit (what a friend!). He was patient under provocation. When he was reviled, he did not pay back in kind. When he was unfairly blamed, he did not answer back. When he was accused, he did not defend himself. He was wondrously free from the lust of self-vindication. When he suffered, he did not threaten to get revenge. Perhaps his assailants mistook his silence for weakness. If they had applied this strategy in their own lives, they would have found it was not weakness but instead supernatural strength![16]

The pain we experience in the workplace does not have the power to destroy us; it can, however, send us straight into the arms of Jesus. Hurting women who have endured hard times, painful rejections, and embarrassment only get ushered into the glorious presence of God by those circumstances if they will be open to that possibility.

God may allow you to be cast down, but he will never destroy you; therefore, learn to sit at his feet and worship him through the Word.

> I have told you these things, so that in Me you may have (perfect) peace and confidence. In the world you have tribulation and trials and distress and frustration; but be of good cheer (take courage; be confident, certain, undaunted)! For I have overcome the world (I have deprived it of power to harm you and have conquered it for you).
>
> John 16:33, TAB

The purpose of this conversation with the disciples was that they might have peace. Jesus knew they would be hated, pursued, persecuted, falsely condemned, and even tortured, so he wanted them to know they could have peace in him. Despite their tribulations, they could rest assured that they were on the winning side.[17]

When I was a hurting woman going through the process of emotional and spiritual recovery, I had to learn how to do what Paul says in Philippians: "Forgetting what lies behind and straining forward to what lies ahead, I press on toward the goal to win the [supreme and heavenly] prize to which God in Christ Jesus is calling us upward" (Philippians 3:13–14, TAB).

Through my spiritual revelation, I finally realized that God had allowed tragedy, struggles, and rejections to come into my life in order to call me into my true purpose. He had a greater plan for my life than anything I had known before, but it was only through isolation and loneliness that I stopped long enough to hear God's voice and learn what he was ready to birth within me for my life and for the good of his kingdom.

I have learned to rejoice when facing trials and unexpected circumstances, because most of the time, God's ultimate plan for my life is being revealed through them. If this sounds like I am describing your life, know that you are highly favored and blessed when God allows pain to come into your life. So many people ask, "Why me, God?" But I have learned to say, "Thank you, God; I know this situation will work out for my good and for your glory."

> Lean on, trust in, and be confident in the LORD with all of your heart and mind and do not rely on your own insight or understanding. In all your ways know, recognize, and acknowledge Him, and He will direct and make straight and plain your paths.
>
> Proverbs 3:5–6, TAB

First, there must be a full commitment of ourselves—spirit, soul, and body—to the Lord. We must trust him not only for the salvation of our souls but also for the direction of our lives. This must be a commitment made without any hesitation. Next, there must be a healthy distrust of self, an acknowledgment that we do not know what is best for us and that we are not capable of guiding ourselves. Finally, there must be an acknowledgment of the Lordship of Christ: "In all your ways acknowledge Him, and He shall direct your paths" (Proverbs 3:6, NKJV). Every area of our lives must be turned over to his control. We must have no will of our own, only a single pure desire to know his will and to do it.[18]

When you are at your lowest and the world has driven you to your closet, remember that both your deliverance *and* your destiny are being molded. "Yet, O Lord, You are our Father; we are the clay, And You our Potter, and we all are the work of Your hand" (Isaiah 64:8, TAB).

God knows all the pain that a hurting woman may be carrying around in her bosom; that is why in Psalm 139:1–4 the psalmist says, "O Lord, you have searched me (thoroughly) and know me. You know my downsitting and my uprising; You understand my thoughts afar off. You sift and search out my path and my lying down, and you are acquainted with all my ways. For there is not a word in my tongue (still unuttered), but, behold, O Lord, You know it altogether."

God is always with us; his presence is always there comforting and healing us. He has declared, "I will not in any way fail you nor give you up nor leave you without support. I will not in any degree leave you helpless nor forsake you nor let you down" (Hebrews 13:5, AMP).

We can face all of our trials, hurdles, and disappointments if we always remember that even while we are in our desert experience, God is always near to offer us a drink of his living water so that we may never thirst again.

He who believes in Me (who cleaves to and trusts in and relies on Me) as the Scripture has said, from his innermost being shall flow (continuously) springs and rivers of living water.

John 7:38, TAB

This verse proves that to come to Christ and drink is the same as to believe in him. All who believe in him will have their own needs supplied and will receive rivers of spiritual blessing that will flow out from them to others. All through the Old Testament it was taught that those who accepted the Messiah would be helped themselves and would become channels of blessing to others (Isaiah 55:1). The expression "out of his heart will flow rivers of living water" means out of a person's innermost being would flow streams of help to others. We drink in small gulps or sips, but those are multiplied into a mighty confluence of flowing streams. We are warned: "No one can be indwelt by the Spirit of God and keep that Spirit to himself. Where the Spirit is, He flows forth; if there is no flowing forth, He is not there."[19]

When we have been hurt by someone else, this forces our defense mechanism to go into high gear, and we immediately begin to search for ways to ensure that no one will ever hurt us again. We get to the point where we'll protect ourselves by any means necessary. We hide our emotions for safekeeping within the safety deposit box of our minds and hearts. We stop living and responding to things spontaneously; we become like artificial flowers on a dining room table.

> We stop living and responding to things spontaneously; we become like artificial flowers on a dining room table.

If you're currently struggling with these very feelings, know that your willingness to forgive and let go of the pain is the only way to walk away from the victim's seat and to not let those who hurt you serve you a life sentence of crippled emotions. You must become your own judge and jury and say, "I have spent enough time in the pity seat; it is time to move on and live in the present."

I don't want to give the impression that I have "arrived" and am totally free from hurt, but I've learned that healing is a process. I still struggle with keeping my mind stayed on Christ even though I am now a lot stronger in him. Prior to surrendering my life to Christ, I was a broken mess. I was so emotionally unstable and insecure, and I was full of fear. But through faith, my life was transformed into something great, and God put his Word in my heart and on my tongue that I could be used by him to bless others. To have consistent victory as a Christian, you must study the Word.

> I have hidden your word in my heart that I might not sin against you.
>
> Psalm 119:11, NIV

A Sunday Prayer in
Preparation for the Workweek

Good Morning, Jesus! I slow myself down for a moment to realize and feel your presence. Today is Sunday, and I welcome you into my workplace to allow your spirit to sit on me until I can execute all tasks without mistakes.

Thank you for my job, and may I find happiness in all of its toil and difficulty; its pleasure and success; its failure and sorrow.

Today is Sunday, dear Lord, and tomorrow starts my workweek. It's time to surrender all to you. I offer to You in praise the words of this beloved hymn:

"All to Jesus I surrender;
All to him I freely give.
I will ever love and trust him;
In his presence daily live.
I surrender all, I surrender all;
All to thee, my blessed Savior,
I surrender all."

Jesus, as I walk to my desk tomorrow, help me to remember that I can't change my past or what happened last week in the workplace. But if I rely on you, my present circumstance and the ones in my future will be handled and changed by you.

Concerning the mistakes, choices, and decisions I made last week that were bad, please forgive me.

Let me walk more holy this week in the workplace.
Let the teaching I received this Sunday at church
stay with me all during the week, so that when I exit
through the church doors, I truly depart to serve.

"All to Jesus I surrender,
Humbly at his feet I bow.
Worldly pleasures all forsaken,
Take me Jesus, take me now.
I surrender all, I surrender all;
All to thee, my blessed Savior,
I surrender all."

Let my light shine this week in the workplace so
that men and women will repent of their sins. Let
me lead others to you through my example. Touch
my mind so that it remains strong. Touch my mouth
so that my words edify others, and touch my heart
so that it reaches out to everyone who is in need.

As I close my prayer, Holy Spirit, please reside in me.
I'm depending on you to see me through this workweek.
You know my needs and my desires. Lead and direct
me into everything that is good and perfect. Strengthen
me to accomplish every task that is assigned to me in
the workplace. Help me not to faint when challenges
come my way. Help me to recall your words so that I
am able to work to the glory of God and not man.

Father, in the name of Jesus, I ask that your grace
and mercy be extended to all the women in my
workplace today. Let not greed, selfishness, or a
paycheck cause us to forget that the things most

important in the work environment are free: love, laughter, caring, and sharing. Let me not forget to work unto you for your glory and not for man's.

In Jesus' name I pray, amen!

Chapter 2

The Job Description of a Hurting Woman in the Workplace

Jane was a remarkable executive assistant who was well liked by everyone in her department. She was also a single mom who shuffled many roles and responsibilities. Jane loved her children, but they were not the center of her life. Jane did not graduate from college but had the potential to become a great leader in her department. Jane had several odd jobs before landing a major professional job in one of the leading industries in her community; however, Jane's self-destructive behavior compensated for her self-doubt and lack of self-love that led to many problems in the workplace. Jane started out as an excellent executive assistant who was devoted to her job, her supervisor, and her teammates. Then about a year into Jane's job, as an executive assistant, her personal dissatisfaction with life began to interrupt her professional life. Her dissatisfaction with life was displayed through Jane becoming more aggressive with her boss, who worked very hard to promote Jane to the next level in the company because she saw her giftness with people. Jane started coming in late for work and sometimes would appear at work not properly dressed.

Jane's boss discussed with Jane her unwelcome behavior in the workplace and encouraged her to get counseling. Little did her boss know, but at one time Jane was homeless. Her parents divorced when she was very young, and her mother bounced around from city to city until Jane was a senior in high school.

Clearly, Jane was making bad choices at work and in her personal life because she was torn between being delivered but had not yet been liberated. She wanted her new life and sense of freedom, but she was stuck in her past and was afraid to enter into her promised land just like the Israelites. Before Jane finally quit her job, she made the comment that her co-workers were trying to coach her into a lifestyle she was not ready to embrace. Jane felt like a scarlet woman, and through all of her success at work she still could not bring herself to believe and accept that she was a treasured woman of God. Everyone was hurt because they wanted so much for Jane to succeed in the workplace, but Jane was a hurting woman who could not mask her pain in the workplace. What Jane was seeking at work could only be obtained through God's Word. The pain that ran fast through Jane's heart like wheels on an Amtrak train will only stop when she arrives at God's destination for her life.

Beloved, do not be amazed and bewildered at the fiery ordeal which is taking place to test your quality, as though something strange (unusual and alien to you and your position) were befalling you. But insofar as you are sharing Christ's sufferings, rejoice, so that when His glory (full of radiance and splendor) is revealed, you may also rejoice with triumph (exultantly). If you are censured and suffer abuse (because you bear) the name of Christ, blessed (are you—happy, fortunate, to be envied, with life—joy, and satisfaction in God's favor and salvation, regardless of your outward condition), because the Spirit of glory, the Spirit of God, is resting upon you. On their part He is blasphemed, but on your part He is glorified.

1 Peter 4:12–14, TAB

Hindsight is 20/20, and that is so true when it comes to identifying and weeding out hurting women in the workplace before you make a job offer to someone. Because hurting women have been living with their pain for so long, they are good at masking their feelings and troubled minds. Some hurting women are alive physically, but their spirits are dead emotionally and spiritually from years of unreleased grief and pain. Hurting women can hide their pain behind a strong outward appearance: they dress successfully, speak with proper grammar, know all the right things to say in an interview, and have college degrees. It is only after your intimate interaction with them in the workplace setting that you will begin to see behaviors and performances that are not a part of the job description established by your organization. Also, most companies are not equipped to deal with hurting women. (At the end of this book I offer some strategies as well as some suggestions to help managers cope with hurting women who are under their supervision.)

Many hurting women are gifted and talented, but

they will never know their full potential because of the enemy within and the inability to stop the rage against themselves.

> Many hurting women are gifted and talented, but they will never know their full potential because of the enemy within and the inability to stop the rage against themselves.

I was once told by a social worker that all feelings are in reference to self; whenever we say something about another person, whether positive or negative, we are actually identifying traits in ourselves.

Hurting women often act like Dr. Jekyll and Ms. Hyde in the workplace. Some days they are calm and cooperative, but on other days when the pain of hiding their insecurities gets to be too much to bear and they need a punching bag to ease that pain, they display self-centeredness and rebelliousness.

Hurting women can't be easily spotted based on stereotypes; they don't necessarily come to work dressed in mini-skirts, but often are nicely groomed with perfectly coiffed hairstyles and wearing classic business attire. Hurting women go to the extreme to be respectable, because they want praise from others and to feel like they are in control in the workplace.

Hurting women gravitate to religious settings disguised in their best Sunday-go-to-meeting clothes. Their critical attitudes in the workplace are passed off as "spiritual discernment." They use flattery in order to score brownie points with the boss. They secretly hope to be admired, a feeling that is covered up by the false humility in which they cloak themselves in the workplace. If their mask were to be taken off, however, you would see what they are really up to.

Discernment is more than just knowing right from wrong; it is about judging a person's behavior accurately and clearly. Scripture tells us that we are to "test all things, hold fast what is good. Abstain from every form of evil" (1 Thessalonians 5:21–22, TAB). What we have to recognize about discernment is that we must weigh the message against the scriptures. We have to make sure someone is not trying to manipulate the situation for gain by proclaiming a "prophetic word" over our life.

> They do all their works to be seen of men.
>
> Matthew 23:5, TAB

The Believer's Bible Commentary supports this when it says,

> They went through religious observances to be seen by men, not from inward sincerity. Their use of phylacteries was an example. In commanding Israel to bind His words as a sign upon their hands and as frontlets between their eyes (Exodus 13:9, 16; Deuteronomy 6:8; 11:18), God meant that the law should continually be before them, guiding their activities. They reduced this spiritual command to a literal, physical sense. Enclosing portions of scripture in leather capsules, they bound them to their foreheads or arms. They weren't concerned about obeying the law as long

as, by wearing ridiculously large phylacteries, they appeared super-spiritual.[20]

Because of their past rejections, hurting women feel that even Jesus Christ will reject them. The hurt that occurred during their childhood still visits them in adulthood. They operate in an adult world with a child's perspective and approval mentality. Hurting women are living with a lot of shame and guilt. What hurting women don't realize is that the people who hurt them were not plugged into the right source but instead were stuck in their own cycle of unresolved pain.

> For (the Spirit which) you have now received (is) not a spirit of slavery to put you once more in bondage to fear, but you have received the Spirit of adoption (the Spirit producing sonship) in (the bliss of) which we cry, Abba (father)! Father! The Spirit Himself (thus) testifies together with our own spirit, (assuring us) that we are children of God. And if we are (his) children, then we are (His) heirs also: heirs of God and fellow heirs with Christ (sharing His inheritance with Him); only we must share his suffering if we are to share His glory. (But what of that?) For I consider that the sufferings of his present time (this present life) are not worth being compared with the glory that is about to be revealed to us and in us for us and conferred on us!
>
> Romans 8:15–18, TAB

Those who live under the law are like children, allowing themselves to be bossed around as if they were servants, their lives constantly overshadowed by the fear of punishment. But when a person is born again, he or she is not born into a position of servitude. He or she is not brought into God's household as a slave but rather receives the spirit of adoption. By true spiritual instinct we can look up to God and call him "Abba, Father." Abba is an Aramaic word that is an intimate form of the word *father*, such as "papa" or "daddy." The God of the universe who is infinitely high above all things is also near to us at all times.[21]

A typical job description lists the required duties a person must perform in order to hold that particular position. For example, there may be a position summary, evaluation and training requirement, and special knowledge, skills, and abilities. When interviewing to fill an open position, we are often more concerned with finding people who have the skills to perform the job rather than focusing on personal traits and how trainable a person might be. Of course this is gradually changing over time, and more and more companies are looking for people who are trainable rather than searching for someone whose résumé and background perfectly matches the ideal candidate for that position.

If I had to write a help-wanted ad for a hurting woman, it would read something like this:

HELP WANTED

Looking for a female of any race who may be single, married, or divorced; educated and/or uneducated; one who has experience as being the lead hurting woman in the workplace. She must have years of living with insecurity and unresolved emotions. She must feel that the only way to be validated is to hurt others. She must be willing to work forty hours a week without experiencing one moment of peace during her workweek. She must never say anything positive about her co-workers and supervisors. She must be able to mask her feelings and create chaos in the workplace. She must dress appropriately, but she also must be emotionally unhappy and have children who are unhappy. She must never admit that she is hurting and must not be willing to forgive others. Purpose-driven women need not apply.

I know this may sound a little humorous, but every day we hire people in the workplace who have these types of issues. If I had to write a job description for the hurting woman, it would be summarized like this:

POSITION SUMMARY OF A HURTING WOMAN

Hurting woman needed to inflict pain and hurt onto others. Must conduct assessment of co-workers' strengths and weaknesses but never assess her own shortcomings. Must address/express needs in the workplace by having a negative attitude toward customers and co-workers. Must be willing to sabotage all teamwork efforts. In addition, the hurting woman will make home visits to other co-workers' homes to lay out plans to disrespect other people in the workplace and will not take advantage of community resources available to help her because she likes living in isolation.

If I had to describe the education and training requirements for a hurting woman's job, it would be summarized like this:

EDUCATION AND TRAINING REQUIREMENTS FOR A HURTING WOMAN:

Education and Experience

- Single, divorced, or looking for a mate

- Prefer a minimum of three to five years living with unresolved emotional issues

- Extensive knowledge is required in having a negative attitude

- No interpersonal and/or communication skills needed

- Inability to understand and communicate the interrelatedness of body, mind, and spirit and how this relates to spiritual growth

- Experience working as the leading hurting woman

If I had to write the special knowledge, skills, and abilities required for the position of hurting woman, it would be summarized like this:

SPECIAL KNOWLEDGE, SKILLS, AND ABILITIES A HURTING WOMAN NEEDS

1. The ability to display intense emotions—tears, anger, bitterness, frustration, and sarcasm.

2. The ability to share very intimate details about her personal life with whomever will listen in the workplace.

3. Skilled at judging others in the workplace. Must be able to complete her duties quickly so she can have extra time to sit on the sidelines and judge others.

4. Must be skilled at avoiding taking on extra duties so that she has time for gossiping with other co-workers. She must be talented at complaining that she has a lot to do, but in reality she wants more time to sing her sad songs to anyone who will listen.

5. Must be competent at envying her co-workers.

6. Must have talent in creating an agenda that tears other people down.

7. Must possess a feeling of emptiness.

8. Must be insecure and able to become angry very easily if criticized.

9. A hurting woman must be skilled at criticizing her co-workers but be unable to make clear and direct decisions concerning her own life.

10. A hurting woman must be able to grumble and complain and grab from others instead of giving.

Hurting women hurt others because they lack a relationship with God. Instead of trusting God they trust in their own instincts and believe that by manipulating and destroying others they will find their true purpose. The job skills mentioned above are characteristics of hurting women in the workplace who might even attend church regularly.

We should desire to fulfill God's job description and attributes as described in Galatians 5:22–23: "The fruit of the spirit is love, joy, peace, patience, kindness, goodness, faithfulness, gentleness, and self control. Against such things there is no law" (TAB).

All of us at some point and time in our work life have fallen out of the grace of God and have bruised other women. The fall normally comes when we are not tuned in to God's plan for our lives. We must watch when the yellow caution light comes on in our lives to prevent ourselves from falling. How can we know when the caution light is warning us that we've gotten off track? When we find ourselves gossiping too much, no longer studying God's Word, attending church sporadically or not at all, and not praying consistently.

> Therefore, let him who thinks he stands take heed lest he fall.
>
> 1 Corinthians 10:12, KJV

God, through the Holy Spirit, can be our mental health counselor. He can use the Holy Spirit to remind us of every good thing he promised to give us if we will just walk out of the darkness and into the light.

> But the Comforter (Counselor, Helper, Intercessor, Advocate, Strengthener, Standby), the Holy Spirit, whom the Father will send in my name (in my place, to represent me and act on My behalf), He will teach you all things. And he will cause you to recall (will remind you of, bring to your remembrance) everything I have told you.
>
> John 14:26, TAB

For all the hurting women reading this, I hope your spirit leaps at the realization that the Holy Spirit is everything. The Holy Spirit will comfort you, walk beside you, and reside in you.

Some of you may have been hurting for so many years that you feel unworthy or undeserving of God's grace. Jesus can heal and restore broken women. This is truly evident in the story of the woman who had the issue of blood.

> And, behold, there was a woman which had a spirit of infirmity eighteen years, and was bowed together, and could in no wise lift up herself. And when Jesus saw her, he called her to him, and said unto her, Woman, thou art loosed from thine infirmity. And he laid his hands on her: and immediately she was made straight, and glorified God.
>
> Luke 13:11–13, KJV

The real attitude of Israel toward the Lord Jesus is seen in the ruler of the synagogue. This official objected that the Savior had healed a woman on the Sabbath. The woman had suffered from severe curvature of the spine for eighteen years. Her deformity was great; she could not straighten herself up at all. Without even being asked, the Lord Jesus had spoken the healing word, had laid his hands on her, and had straightened her spine.[22]

> Also, we can see Jesus' willingness to heal the blind beggar, but his request to the young man was, "Do you want to be made whole?"

In these lay a great number of sick folk—some blind, some crippled, and some paralyzed (shriveled up)—waiting for the bubbling up of the water. For an angel of the Lord went down at appointed seasons into the pool and moved and stirred up the water; whoever then first, after the stirring up of the water stepped in was cured of whatever disease with which he was afflicted. There was a certain man there who had suffered with a deep-seated and lingering disorder for thirty-eight years. When Jesus noticed him lying there (helpless), knowing that he had already been a long time in that condition, He said to him, Do you want to become well? (Are you really in earnest about getting well?)

John 5:3–6, TAB

Apparently the pool of Bethesda was known as a place where miracles of healing occurred. Whether these miracles took place throughout the year, or only at certain times, such as on feast days, we do not know. Surrounding the pool were a large number of sick people who had come with the hope of being cured. Some were blind, others lame, and still others were paralyzed. These various types of infirmity picture sinful man in his helplessness, blindness, lameness, and uselessness.

These people, suffering from the effect of sin in their bodies, were waiting for the moving of the water. Their hearts were filled with longing to be freed from their sicknesses, and they earnestly desired to find healing.

In loving compassion, he said to him, "Do you want to be made well?" Jesus knew that this was the greatest longing of the man's heart. But he also wanted to draw out from the man an admission of his own helplessness and of his desperate need for healing. It is much the same with salvation.

The Lord knows that we desperately need to be saved, but he waits to hear the confession from our own lips that we lost, that we need him and accept him as our Savior. We are not saved by our own will, yet the human will must be exercised before God saves a soul.[23]

Being able to identify hurting women in the workplace should help us minister to them and not judge them in any way. When we judge another person, we immediately establish a wall between them and us that sometimes will never be torn down unless the other person perceives that we really do care about them and are not just learning information about them in order to gossip. When we judge people too quickly and too harshly simply because they have made a mistake or because we are having a bad day, we miss out on opportunities to develop good friends, enjoy good conversations, and build lasting memories.

Christian women are to be extremely focused in the workplace to identify the hurting women around them and to reach out to them by inviting them to church or sharing a positive word. However, what I have seen with a lot of Christian women in the workplace is that they separate themselves from these hurting women. They fear "assimilation by association," but Jesus said that he came to heal the sick, and he instructed us to do likewise. Christian women also need to guard themselves against getting caught up in gossiping and interfering with these hurting women because, as we all know, meddling is not always for the good of the other person but instead is meant to tear down and destroy her.

I have seen nuns, priests, ministers, and men of the cloth pass out judgment in the workplace; they assumed that because they were saved, their lives were flawless and they were more worthy than the hurting women. We Christians tend to dish out words and display actions as to who we think deserves God's mercy, but he says that no one is good but the Father.

We Christians are called to live *in* the world even though we are not *of* the world. We are not to separate ourselves from other people and discriminate against them, but rather, we are to construct bridges to other people's hearts to influence them for the gospel and bring them to Jesus Christ.

God is the only one who can deliver us from unexpected pain and betrayal. David provided us with evidence of this in Psalm 62:1–2, 5–8 (KJV):

> Truly my soul waiteth upon God: from him cometh my salvation. He only is my rock and my salvation; he is my defense; I shall not be greatly moved. How long will ye imagine mischief against a man? Ye shall be slain all of you: as a bowing wall shall ye be, and a tottering fence. They only consult to cast him down from his excellency: they delight in lies; they bless with their mouth, but they curse inwardly. My soul, wait thou only upon God; for my expectation is from him. He only is my rock and my salvation: he is my defense; I shall not be moved. In God is my salvation and my glory: the rock of my strength and my refuge is God. Trust in him at all times; ye people, pour out your heart before him: God is a refuge for us.

Gwen now has her PhD in education after more than twenty years as an elementary school teacher. Gwen is a high achiever. Her students love her and think that Gwen is one of the most gifted teachers that has walked the halls of Haven Elementary School. Gwen is a super Sunday school teacher, math teacher, and very community minded. However, every day Gwen goes to work she is participating in a masquerade because she has no true identity. Her identity is defined by her many external roles.

Because of her identity crisis, Gwen is addicted to drama in the workplace. She causes much strife and contention in her teaching ward, and her co-workers avoid her in the teachers' lounge. Gwen thinks they avoid her because they are jealous of her accomplishments. Gwen dramatizes every situation at work and turns small problems into giant molehills. She takes everything very seriously and shares few laughs with her co-workers.

Gwen's heart is a broken mess that only God can fix. Gwen hides her pain like frequent lightning during a severe thunderstorm. Gwen's father died in a car accident when she was only nine, and she has never shed a tear over the sudden loss in her life. Gwen's mother raised her and her young brother on a waitress's salary. Gwen did not experience much happiness as a child and was alone most of the time, tending to her younger brother while her mother worked long hours to pay the bills. Gwen was always encouraged by her mother to be a grownup when she desired to go outside and be a kid like her friends next door.

Christmas and Thanksgiving were the only days Gwen was truly happy because her mother did not work and the entire family got a chance to be together. Gwen was a good student in high school and was encouraged by her teachers to go college, which is one reason she entered the teaching profession. Gwen was engaged for a brief time after college, but her fiancé broke off the engagement two weeks before the wedding.

Gwen is a loving woman, but her painful feelings from earlier years are locked away in her mind like a prisoner behind a locked gate. Gwen crusades through the school hallways like an embalmed bodied but not yet buried. Gwen's coworkers describe Gwen as someone whose feelings are like dry leaves blowing on autumn school days.

A Prayer for Monday in the Workplace

Good Morning, Jesus! I slow myself down for a
moment so that I may sense your presence. Today
is Monday, and I welcome you into my workplace to allow your spirit to rest on me so that
I may execute all tasks without mistakes.

I pray that you will give me patience and strength to
deal with my busy workplace where things sometimes
feel like they are moving at the speed of an Amtrak
train. This often involves too many meetings, hall-
way conferences, and a flood of unread e-mails.

In the midst of this busyness, let me find a quiet time
to draw near to you so that I do not lose my Christian character. Help me to use my lunch break to
retreat to a quiet place, even if that quiet place is in the
bathroom and/or in my car, where I can rest in your
presence and be strengthened for what lies ahead.

Let me be renewed every morning this week, because
great is your faithfulness. Amid mental, emotional,
and physical suffering let my co-workers find con-
solation in your healing presence within me. Show
your love as you heal wounds, destroy illnesses,
mend broken hearts, and free downcast spirits.

As I close my prayer, Holy Spirit, please reside in me.
I'm depending on you to see me through this workday.
You know my needs and my desires. Lead and direct me
into everything that is good and perfect. Strengthen me

to accomplish every task that is assigned to me today in the workplace. Help me not to feel overcome when challenges arrive. Help me to recall your words that I am to work for the glory of God and not for man.

In Jesus' name I pray, amen!

Chapter 3
How a Hurting Woman Operates in the Workplace

Tamara was a young lady who, for the first time since she had graduated from college, finally landed a job in her field of study. Prior to accepting the position as the manager for special programs, Tamara had worked in dead-end jobs with no real chance for promotion. However, when she took the position as a manager for a company that had more than six thousand employees, she finally felt complete.

Very soon Tamara began to compare herself to her accomplished supervisor who had been in the field for more than seventeen years. Tamara was well liked by her female supervisor, who was coaching and mentoring Tamara for a higher position. But Tamara's unresolved issues from her childhood and her relationship with her drug-abusing mother and her own brief period of teenage experimentation with drugs led her to secretly practice sabotaging behavior in the workplace. Tamara began to talk about her supervisor with other co-workers. She presented herself to others in charge as being the person who was responsible for anything good that came out of her department, even though her supervisor was on the ground floor with all planned activities.

Tamara's supervisor did not realize that Tamara was trying to take her position until they had a disagreement about how a project should be completed. Tamara's boss had been very supporting of Tamara through all of her family conflict, a separation from her husband, then a divorce, and was her primary champion, encouraging Tamara to go back to school and to work on her master's degree. Tamara, who became frustrated because she could not replace her supervisor, eventually moved on, but her pain lingers. The healing of Tamara's pain will only come just like the medicine in a balm leaf; once God's aloe is spread across Tamara's body and mind, it will penetrate her hard heart and release a new way of living and responding to life. Wherever Tamara is today, we pray her healing has begun.

> Come unto me, all ye that labor and are heavy laden, and I will give you rest. Take my yoke upon you, and learn of me; for I am meek and lowly in heart: and ye shall find rest unto your souls. For my yoke is easy, and my burden is light.
>
> Matthew 11:28–30, KJV

Hurting women normally operate superficially in the workplace. They operate in falsehood and self-deception. Everything about a hurting woman in the workplace is counterfeit because they are not living out the life they were created to live. The reason why many women are operating foolishly in the workplace is because they lack knowledge and wisdom. Proverbs teaches us that wisdom provides a future of hope.

My son, eat honey, because it is good, and the drippings of the honeycomb are sweet to your taste. So shall you know skillful and godly wisdom to be thus to your life; if you find it, then shall there be a future and a reward, and your hope and expectation shall not be cut off. Lie not in wait as a wicked man against the dwelling of the (uncompromisingly) righteous (the upright, in right standing with God); destroy not his resting place; For a righteous man falls seven times and rises again, but the wicked are over thrown by calamity.

Proverbs 24: 13–16, TAB

Honey is used here as a symbol of wisdom because it is beneficial and sweet to the taste; so shall the knowledge of wisdom be to your soul. Once you have found wisdom, your hope will not be cut off. The woman who finds wisdom is assured of a bright future and the realization of all her hopes.[24]

Hurting women can really put on a performance in the workplace. They can operate within the guidelines of the organization without putting themselves at risk of being fired, but they push the envelope with their behavior by working right up to the edge that borders between breaking the rules and not breaking them.

Hurting women prey on the sympathy of their female bosses by using the universal maternal instincts that women have for protecting their children. When I was in a management position, so many times I fell into the trap of women manipulating me because of my compassion and desire to help others and my propensity to see the good in everyone. Hurting women tell stories to their "mother hen" bosses about how their child is misbehaving at school; how the husband and/or boyfriend is cheating on them; how they did not grow up with their mother or father; how they did not get a college education because they dropped out of school early; how they want to go back to school but can't because they have such a heavy workload; how they're working to put their husband through school; how they got pregnant and the father is not in the child's life; and the list goes on and on.

However, after many painful experiences and getting burned so many times by the lies told to me by hurting women, I have been able to identify patterns of their behavior that I am now sharing in this book. As you read this book, you may find yourself in these pages, but I would challenge you not to let that embarrass or shame you into not reading further; instead, be encouraged and keep reading, for there is help within these pages all the way to the end of the book.

In order to rise up to your fullest potential in the workplace you must first recognize how you operate in that environment. Determining how you operate in the workplace on a regular basis lies in the answer to the following question: Are you making a valuable contribution, or are you using the workplace as a therapist's office to try and work out your problems without the expense of paying a psychologist? Many times in my role as a supervisor, I was cornered into having counseling sessions with my female employees, which made it harder to address deficits they may have had in performing their regular job duties.

Hurting women in the workplace often are trying

to serve two masters. They are enslaved to the master of emotional bondage, and they are enslaved to the master of wanting sympathy from others because of their past wounds. They want to be set free, but they get an emotional high from being able to say their life is a mess, they have been through so much, and they want to make sure everyone can see their pain. But God is saying that we must press toward the mark of the high calling we have in Jesus Christ.

> No man can serve two masters; for either he will hate the one, and love the other; or else he will hold to the one, and despise the other. Ye cannot serve God and mammon.
>
> Matthew 6:24, KJV

I love the way the *Believer's Bible Commentary* discusses this verse in Matthew:

> The impossibility of living for God and for money is stated here in terms of masters and slaves. No one can serve two masters. One will inevitably take precedence in his loyalty and obedience. So it is with God and mammon. They present rival claims and a choice must be made. Either we must put God first and reject the rule of materialism or we must live for temporal things and refuse God's claim on our lives.[25]

Most women let their problems become the master of their daily lives, and thus they become slaves to negative thinking. They get up in the morning worrying about the past, and they lie down at night pondering the future; then they wake up the next morning talking about what happened yesterday, repeating the cycle endlessly. They even operate like this in the workplace. They worry about their co-workers' behaviors. They allow their relationships with their supervisors to be defined by constant fear and confusion.

As hurting women, if we would just walk out of the past and into the bright future that God has planned for us, we would understand that he does not want us to worry about our lives. He does not want us to be anxious for anything.

> Therefore I say unto you, Take no thought for your life, what ye shall eat, or what you shall drink; nor yet for your body, what ye shall put on. Is not the life more than meat, and the body than rainment? Behold the fowls of the air; for they sow not, neither do they reap, nor gather into barns; yet your heavenly Father feedeth them. Are ye not much better than they? Which of you by taking thought can add one cubit unto his stature?
>
> Matthew 6: 25–27, KJV

In this passage, Jesus strikes at the tendency to center our lives on food and clothing, thus missing life's real meaning. The problem is not so much what we eat and wear today, but what we shall eat and wear ten, twenty, or thirty years from now. Such worry about the future is sin because it denies the love, wisdom, and power of God. It denies the love of God by implying that he doesn't care for us. It denies his wisdom by implying that he doesn't know what he is doing. And it denies his power by implying that he isn't able to provide for our needs.

This type of worry causes us to devote our finest energies to making sure we will have enough to live on. Then before we know it, our lives have passed, and we have missed the central purpose for which we were made. God did not create us in his image with no higher destiny than that we should consume food. We are here to love, worship, and serve him and to represent his interests on earth. Our bodies are intended to be our servants, not our masters.

The birds of the air illustrate God's care for his creatures. They preach to us how unnecessary it is for us to worry. They neither sow nor reap, yet God feeds them. Since, in God's hierarchy of creation, we are of more value than the birds, then we can surely expect God to take care of our needs.

But we should not infer from this that we need not work for the supply of our present needs. Paul reminds us: "If anyone will not work, neither shall he eat" (2 Thessalonians 3:10). Nor should we conclude that it is wrong for a farmer to sow, reap, and harvest.[26]

We should not be anxious and operate in the workplace with fear in our hearts, because our lives will not be extended by incessant worrying. Jesus knows what it's like to cope with pain in the workplace. He knows and sympathizes with us when we are wounded by people who should have stayed up with us praying and watching instead of hurting us. In performing his earthly job duties, Jesus sometimes experienced moments of emotional breakdown. Sometimes his grief was so unbearable that it made him weep.

> And when he was come near, he beheld the city, and wept over it. Saying, if thou hadst known, even thou, at least in this thy day, the things which belong unto thy peace! but now they are hid from thine eyes. For the days shall come upon thee, that thine enemies shall cast a trench about thee, and compass thee round, and keep thee in on every side.
>
> Luke 19:41–43, KJV

As Jesus drew near to Jerusalem, He uttered a lamentation over the city that had missed its golden opportunity. If the people had only received Him as Messiah, it would have meant peace for them. But they didn't recognize that He was the source of peace. Now it was too late. They had already determined what they would do with the Son of God. Because of their rejection of Him, their eyes were blinded. Because they *would not* see Him, they no longer *could* see Him.[27]

Sometimes when we're dealing with hurting women in the workplace and it seems that our pleading with them to operate differently yields no results, we must keep walking around our office space day after day, modeling the same level of faith that Joshua and the Israelites displayed as they walked around the walls of Jericho. God's ways are not our ways, and his thoughts are not our thoughts.

Satan loves using psychological warfare in the workplace to keep women operating and residing in a state of pain and confusion. He also does this to keep women separated from each other emotionally, because he fears the strength they would find in unity. He makes women gossip about each other and create feelings of insecurity about other women's perceived successes, failures, and weaknesses.

> For where envying and strife is, there is confusion and every evil work. But the wisdom that is from above is first pure, then peaceable, gentle, and easy to be entreated, full of mercy and good fruits, without partiality, and without hypocrisy. And the fruit of righteousness is sown in peace of them that make peace.
>
> James 3:16–18, KJV

Whenever there is an atmosphere of envy and self-seeking, there will also be confusion and disharmony. When we reject true wisdom and act according to our own supposed cleverness, we create a spirit of unrest and agitation, but the wisdom that comes from God is pure and clean in thought, word, and deed. It is undefiled in spirit and body, in doctrine and practice, and in faith and morals. It is also peaceable. This simply means that a wise woman who loves peace will do all she can to maintain that peace within her workplace without sacrificing purity. She must also be willing to yield, letting go of the temptation to be obstinate and adamant about having things her way. When a woman operates within the realm of God's wisdom, she will be full of mercy to those who are in the wrong and anxious to help them find the right way. She will be compassionate and kind, and there will be no vindictiveness in her; indeed, she will reward discourtesy with benevolence, and she will be able to do so without showing partiality or favoritism.[28]

Many women operate in a state of defiance in the workplace because, like Miriam in the Old Testament, it's not that these women are upset because another person is the boss; rather, they are upset because *they* are *not* the boss. Miriam (and her brother Aaron) coveted Moses' position of leadership, and thus they couldn't bring themselves to speak highly of him among the other co-workers. They were very jealous of Moses, and so they did not know how to love him. They were envious of him, which made them unable to receive him as their leader.

So many women today don't like their supervisors in the workplace because they think they can do a better job of being in control. If you are a manager or supervisor, know that not everyone is going to like you, especially because you are in a position of leadership and power. It doesn't matter how you behave, or what you say, or what you think, or what choices you make; somebody is going to dislike you. There will always be a few employees who are going to complain and cause problems.

Actually, Satan loves having hurting women in the workplace, because he knows that he can use these individuals to hinder and destroy the ones in leadership positions. Even Christian women often get used by Satan in the workplace as they get caught up in trying to destroy another person in leadership. Many forget the scripture that says, "Remind your people to submit to rulers and authorities, to obey them, and to be ready to do good in every way. Tell them not to speak evil of anyone, but to be peaceful and friendly, and always to show a gentle attitude toward everyone" (Titus 3:1–2, TAB).

The saddest thing is that many women in the workplace allow evil to creep into their hearts and possess their minds. The evil one tempts women to secretly begin to turn against a good leader by gossiping and scheming, with the hope that they will become the leader by demolishing that person's name or by trying to damage the person's reputation.

Sometimes as hurting women in the workplace, we strive so hard to put on a false performance that we miss the assignment that God placed us there to accomplish in the first place. We make a trip through the workplace, but we miss the spiritual journey.

For Christian women to operate effectively in the workplace, they must have a head-on collision with Christ by saturating themselves with praise and worship. God's Word is alive, and it can ignite our spirits to fly out of the target zone and into the unfriendly territory of unrest, confusion, and disturbance if we would just study and meditate on his Word every day. His Word cannot return to him void.

Many hurting women feel they are in a dead-end job, so they wander around the workplace confused and lost. They have yet to realize that the path they are on is to introduce them to the world of work and to teach them valuable lessons that will be useful later on. For example, through your job, God may be teaching you how to manage money, how to submit to authority, how to get along with other women, how to negotiate a contract, how to finish a difficult task, and so on.

If we would slow down and listen to God's voice, we would realize that the workplace is not just about getting ahead in the world, but it's also a place where we can learn how to live a balanced and spiritual life. The job we hold is God's way of preparing us for the next assignment, and we often miss the lesson currently being taught because we are distracted by trying to hurt others.

Hurting women need to confide in God about every aspect of their lives: their current circumstances and their future direction. But the only way God will confide in us is if we express a holy fear and awe of his greatness. Psalm 25:14 says, "The LORD confides in those who fear him" (TAB). Most women don't fear God—they fear their circumstances. They fear losing their job, their husband, their health, their children, and the list can go on and on. Because we sometimes fear the wrong things, the presence of God is hidden from us.

Hurting women want to get over their pain, but they must first accept it and then be willing to reveal the pain, share the pain with others, and speak the pain by admitting they are hurting. What hurting women have not learned is that they do not have to operate in the workplace with masks on. You don't have to wear a made-up face to get into the presence of God. He wants you to come into his presence just as you are.

We shouldn't be too hasty to seek deliverance, but instead we should ask God to preserve us through the hurt, because it is adversity that shapes our destiny.

As Christian women, God requires that we provide excellent customer service, and this means internal customers as well—our coworkers. This should be our primary task on the clock and off the clock. Providing exceptional customer service will guarantee you a promotion in the heavenly kingdom.

If you make excellent customer service your priority, you will be like a star and it will not be a struggle for you to shine in dark moments. You will be like a river flowing through the workplace and will never struggle to excel in life, because God will grant you the best. Your labor will never be in vain, your plans will never fail, your destiny will not be aborted, and the desire of your heart will be granted in Jesus' name.

Creating an atmosphere of confusion in the workplace in an effort to dull your pain may provide a quick fix, but it will never solve your life's problems; it just postpones the solution. Always remember this eternal truth: "What we hold on to diminishes, and what we let go of multiplies." Pain that is not dealt with can become entrenched in our psyche and develop into a lifestyle that destroys families, relationships, and jobs. Many people will never know true peace until they surrender to God, who holds everything in his hand. As God tries to direct our paths, there is always an enemy at work trying to zap our energy and drown our sprits. We are God's gifts and secret treasures lent to the earth for a short time.

Many women want visible power in the workplace, but true power cannot really be seen. Power is something that, if applied correctly, will produce positive outcomes. Some people use power to hurt others because they fail to understand that power has purpose, and only with the correct application of power will it be useful to the one who uses it. Power executed or interpreted incorrectly in the workplace often comes across in the following attitudes:

> Do it yourself—you're the supervisor.
>
> I did the work, so why are they getting the credit?
>
> I don't care what you think; I am going to do it my way.

I would like to close this chapter with a short essay about haters that was sent to me by e-mail while I was working on this section of the book. I don't know the author, but the content of the essay conveys the point I want to make about how hurting women operate in the workplace:

> A hater is someone who is jealous and envious and spends all her time trying to make you look small so that she can look tall.
>
> When you make your mark, you will always attract some haters…That's why you have to be careful who you share your blessings and your dreams with, because some folks can't handle seeing you blessed.

It's dangerous to be like somebody else ... If God wanted you to be like somebody else he would have given you what he gave them.

You don't know what people have gone through to get what they have ... (the problem I have with haters is that they see my glory, but they don't know my story ...) If the grass looks greener on the other side of the fence, you can rest assured that the water bill is higher there too.

We've all got some haters among us. Some people don't like it that you can:

- come to church.
- get your praise on.
- bless his holy name.

Haters don't want to see you happy. Haters don't want to see you succeed. Haters don't want you to get the victory.

Most of our haters are people who are supposed to be on our side. How do you handle the haters who you at least expect to have your guard up against? You can handle your haters by:

- knowing who you are and who your true friends are.
- having a purpose.
- remembering that what you have is by divine prerogative and not human manipulation.

Purpose does not mean having a job. You can have a job and still be unfulfilled. A purpose is having a clear sense of what God has called you to be. Your purpose is not defined by what others think about you.

You will always be trying to get stuff, because the more stuff you have will improve what others think about you; but what others think will last longer than the stuff lasts.

When God gives you favor, you can tell your haters, "Don't look at me…Look at who is in charge of me."

—Author Unknown

In some hallways where hurting women work every day, the atmosphere is like the aftermath of a hurricane that has ripped through and dramatically leveled the foundation of the women's souls. The debris that is left in the workplace after the stormy emotional outbursts of hurting women can only be removed through the rescue workers and search teams assigned by Jesus. His rescue workers are trained to go under the dangerously unsteady foundation that was destroyed by Satan and gradually begin to remove the rubble.

> In some hallways where hurting women work every day, the atmosphere is like the aftermath of a hurricane that has ripped through and dramatically leveled the foundation of the women's souls.

When we are underneath the rubble in our workplace, we must remember to keep our eyes lifted above and our hands folded and knees bent in constant prayer to God.

Hurting women who have not had an opportunity to express themselves after a devastating loss often operate in the workplace on autopilot, fueled by the adrenaline rush of the survival instinct kicking in gear. Many of them have never stopped and just had a breakdown over all the fatalities their lives have been exposed to. Being a trained social worker, I know that the first step to healing is to begin to talk about the pain.

The hostility that we women can have against each other only serves to alienate us and compromise our integrity, undermining our witness as God-fearing women. The battle will only be won by building a bridge over our painful memories and scars. As children of God, we must march straight out of our pain and into our promised land.

A Prayer for Tuesday in the Workplace

Good Morning, Jesus! I slow myself down for a moment so that I may sense your presence. Today is Tuesday, and I welcome you into my workplace to allow your spirit to rest on me until I can execute all tasks without mistakes.

I pray that you would help me to hear what the Holy Spirit says to me in the workplace today and not just what bosses and co-workers are saying.

Speak to me about the future, dear Lord, and help me not be led by everyone else. Help me realize that future successes do not depend on past mistakes, but on what I do each day, as long as I maintain a positive mind-set.

Help me to avoid negative people. Help me not to complain or grumble but to press through my wilderness in the workplace knowing there is another place for me flowing with milk and honey and every good thing that I could imagine—and with no shortage of anything I need.

Let me have an attitude of gratitude in the workplace. Let me look up from the position that I currently hold and, like Abraham, see where you want to take me. I will lift up my eyes and look northward, southward, eastward, and westward, and I will continually be ready to go wherever you lead me.

As I close my prayer, I would ask you, Holy Spirit, to please reside in me. I'm depending on you to see me through this workday. You know my needs and my desires. Lead and direct me into everything that is good and perfect. Strengthen me to accomplish every task that is assigned to me today in the work-place. Help me not to faint when challenges come my way. Help me to recall your Word where it says that I am to work to the glory of God and not man.

In Jesus' name I pray, amen!

Chapter 4

A Hurting Woman's Struggle for Promotion in the Workplace

Nancy had been living on her own since she was sixteen years old. Her mother had put her out of the house when she became pregnant her junior year in high school. Nancy was a gifted and talented student, so she lived the last two years of high school with the school counselor, who did not want Nancy to drop out of high school. Nancy finished school with high honors, and to escape from her mother, an alcoholic with mental issues, she enlisted in the military. Nancy was happy in the military because she got to move around, meet new people, and put her last two years of high school behind her. She was able to locate good childcare facilities for her young child, and Nancy was content (or at least she thought). Nancy finally left the army after seven years.

As a youth counselor for the Williams Youth Center, Nancy often shared with co-workers and youth leaders her desire to be a minister. Prior to Nancy accepting the position as youth counselor, she was a childcare worker with the local military base in her hometown. Nancy, who was in the midst of finishing college when she started as the youth counselor, appeared to be very focused on her goals in life. But after two years and degree in hand, Nancy felt the need to be on the leadership track at the youth center, especially since she had been properly trained and coached by her female supervisors.

Satan planted in Nancy's head that how she behaved at work had nothing to do with her everyday Christian walk and her desire to be a minister because, after all, work is work and church is church. So Nancy began to be more aggressive by making decisions that were clearly the decisions that should have been made by her bosses. Nancy kept important phone calls and messages from her bosses and attempted to handle situations without their supervision and guidance to make the point that she was capable of being a leader.

What Nancy's cohorts did not know about Nancy was that she had come to the youth center a broken woman. Nancy had already experienced one failed marriage that ended very painfully and was left with questions about her self-worth as a woman.

However, because most of Nancy's supervisors were women at the youth center, issues that she thought had been put to rest in regards to her mother and neglect resurfaced. The attitudes and behaviors of the women Nancy worked with at the youth center were different from her mother's. Nancy unknowingly reacted aggressively to the female authority over her because of her unresolved issues about parenting.

Nancy's desire to become a minister was valid, but it was also her escape plan to keep from facing unresolved pain. Nancy, feeling out of place at work, decided to move and start her own business, but was short-lived. Nancy is now back in the workplace, still wondering around aimlessly. Hopefully, Nancy will find this book and find her way home to God.

Nothing others do is because of you. What others say and do is a projection of their own reality, their own dream. When you are immune to the opinions and actions of others, you won't be the victim of needless suffering.

—Author Unknown

First, let me open this chapter by saying that we should seek a promotion from our heavenly boss instead of our earthly boss. If God promotes us, then we can never be demoted in the worship place, the church place, or any other place where we reside. Jesus said, "Seek ye first the kingdom of God and His righteousness, and all these things shall be added unto you" (Matthew 6:33, KJV).

When your very existence and validation in the workplace rests totally on whether or not your supervisor appreciates your service, you will experience many days of misery and dissatisfaction. The workplace is not a place to be affirmed. Affirmation should be done at home. When it is not done at home, women come to the workplace seeking promotion and validation.

I have known hurting women who thought they were eligible for promotion even though they regularly participated in gossip, sabotage, and lying, and some of them even put his or her career at risk just to make themselves appear better able to perform the job. I believe in fair competition in the workplace, but I don't endorse the policy that "anything goes" when it comes to getting a promotion.

Many of these women who wanted a promotion were only able to seek advancement because they had been mentored and well-trained by their current bosses, who had taken the women under their wings and showed them the ropes, so to speak.

Hurting women often want titles that they are not yet qualified to hold. They request or demand that they get sent to management-level courses when they really need to be in entry-level continuing-education courses. They want to attend meetings and functions designated for those in management. There is such a common misconception that "If I get the corner office or the biggest office with a great view, then I'll be happy." They don't realize that they only want these things in order to pattern their lives after someone they feel is living the corporate dream. Happiness cannot be bought, however, or bargained for; it is a state of being.

So often these hurting women want a promotion in the workplace for the wrong reasons. They want a promotion to gain new status, which only validates them on the outside; they want what someone else has; they want to hide their emotions and pain by being a workaholic; or they want to gain a title. They want the promotion, but they fail to recognize the responsibilities. My experience has been that even when hurting women receive a raise to compensate for their increased workload, they still complain that they've got too much work to do. They never stop to assess the hard work and sacrifice it takes to be a leader.

There is nothing wrong with wanting a promotion, but many hurting women betray the confidence of others just to get what they want, and when they finally get it, they realize it is not really what they thought it would be, so they continue to hurt others even when they're in a leadership position.

> There is nothing wrong with wanting a promotion, but many hurting women betray the confidence of others just to get what they want, and when they finally get it, they realize it is not really what they thought it would be, so they continue to hurt others even when they're in a leadership position.

Jesus was an ordinary man in the workplace. He did not seek promotion, but instead he went about his daily duties giving glory to God. He was a carpenter born into poverty to a peasant girl in a sandy quiet village that did not always register on the world map ("And Nathaniel said unto him, can there any good thing come out of Nazareth? Philip saith unto him. Come and see" (John 1:46, KJV)). However, he was raised to achieve greatness because of his humbleness and because he let God promote him and not man.

The problem is that many hurting women have masked their pain for so long that they are not moved by the positive gestures, words, and actions of their leaders. This is exactly what the prophet Ezekiel was talking about in Ezekiel 33:31:

> And they come unto thee as the people cometh, and they sit before thee as my people, and they hear thy words, but they will not do them: for with their mouth they show much love, but their heart goeth after their covetousness (KJV).

However, to receive a promotion from God we have to get alone by ourselves, quiet the distracting noise in our head, and listen for him to tell us about our life plan and our destiny.

I am convinced that all of us have an internal magnet that causes us to long for Jesus. Whether we are religious or not, this longing is our heart's deepest treasure. Some people confuse this longing with personal achievement and material things, such as job promotions, houses, cars, jewelry, and riches. These things can never truly fulfill us. Because of the way God wired us spiritually, the only thing that can fulfill us is Jesus Christ. The only person who can truly promote us is God. God will reveal his plan for your life through His spirit.

> As it is written: "No eyes has seen, no ear has heard, no mind has conceived what God has prepared for those who love him"—but God has revealed it to us by his spirit. The spirit searches all things, even the deep things of God. For who among men knows the thoughts of a man except the man's spirit within him? In the same way no one knows the thoughts of God except the spirit of God. We have not received the spirit of the world but the spirit who is from God, that we may understand what God has freely given us.
>
> 1 Corinthians 2:9–14, NIV

The first verse of the above passage is quoting a prophecy from Isaiah 64:4, which tells us that God has treasured up wonderful truths that cannot be discovered by the natural senses but which in due time he will reveal to those who love him. We are unable to receive the things of the spirit of God through our limited human abilities. The only way we can possibly comprehend them is if they are spiritually understood.[29]

If we want a promotion in our jobs, we should seek to understand God more fully. It's one thing to follow God, but it's another to put your complete trust in him. When one person verbally attacks another in the workplace, it is usually because they perceive the other individual as being alone and vulnerable. If you are on the receiving end of such verbal abuse, it's probably because they don't realize you *aren't* vulnerable—and that is because you belong to God; and thus you are never alone.

When you belong to God, you don't need to be validated by a position or title. You don't belong to your circumstances, you don't belong to your job, you don't belong to your children, you don't belong to your parents—but you *do* belong to God.

However, you will never know who you belong to until you stop seeking validation through your work status; instead, seek validation of your status from God, who created you for his glory and calls you his daughter.

> Even everyone that is called by my name: for I have created him for my glory, I have formed him.
>
> Isaiah 43:7, KJV

> This people have I formed for myself; they shall show forth my praise.
>
> Isaiah 43:21, KJV

In tones of tender love, Jehovah assures his people that they need not fear, because he who created, formed, redeemed, and called them will be with them in the flood and in the fire. The Holy One of Israel gives Egypt as their ransom, a promise that was fulfilled after the return of the Jews from captivity. But the exodus is forgettable compared to what he is going to do in the lives of his children now. He will make a road through the desert for his people as they return from captivity. In the renewed earth, the waste places will enjoy plentiful water supplies so that the creatures of the wilderness will be satisfied. God's people, too, will be grateful for the plenty that surrounds them, and they will praise his name.[30]

God wants to give you direction for your life, but he also wants you to follow him once he's given that direction. He knows the outcome of every situation, and if you will let him steer the wheel, he will allow the pathway of your future to unfold before you as you trust him.

An earthly promotion only brings satisfaction for a while. I have seen many hurting women earn promotions, but their lives remain off-key. They are far from fulfilling their purpose and calling. They use their job title and status to hide their brokenness. They never allow anyone to peer into their life once they've officially clocked out after work.

It is okay to be proud of your accomplishments in the workplace, but don't become prideful. Pride will cause you to elevate your thoughts to such a point that you believe you deserve better than what is happening to you.

Pride goes before destruction, and a haughty spirit before a fall

Proverbs 16:18, TAB

Just as lightning usually strikes the tallest trees, so God will put down those who are conceited. Stuck-up people may carry on in that vein for some time, but eventually they will suffer a humiliating experience, one that seems perfectly designed to deflate their ego. It takes only a small pin to prick a large balloon. It was pride that caused the most beautiful angel, Lucifer, to fall from grace and be cast out of heaven, forever renamed Satan. Lucifer had "aspiring pride and insolence for which God threw him from the face of heaven." [31]

Satan appealed to Eve through her pride and the lust of her flesh. He hasn't changed his ways, and he tempts us to justify hurting other women in the workplace by telling us that we will gain more knowledge, insight, and understanding if we step on others as we climb to the top. He manipulates hurting women by convincing them that soon they will have power and authority. There is nothing wrong with desiring more authority, but when it is exercised apart from God's direction, it becomes destructive and unjust.

> And the serpent said unto the woman, "Ye shall not die: For God doth know that in the day ye eat, thereof, then your eyes shall be opened, and ye shall be as gods, knowing good and evil." And when the woman saw that the tree was good for food, and that it was pleasant delight to the eyes, and a tree to be desired to make one wise, she took of the fruit, thereof, and did eat.
>
> Genesis 3:4–6, KJV

Do not love the world, nor the things in the world; if anyone loves the world, the love of the Father is not in him. For all that is in the world—the lust of the flesh, the lust of the eyes, and the boastful pride of life—is not from the Father but is from the world.

When we want an earthly promotion, we should pray about it to God, asking his will for our lives. Praying is making your request known to God. He then answers in accordance with his will. Know that what you are praying for in terms of an earthly promotion may be totally different from what God has designed for you even before you were born. We should not pray to God only to receive blessings, but rather, we should pray to God because he is the Alpha and Omega, the beginning and the end.

> That men ought always to pray, and not lose heart.
>
> Luke 18:1, KJV

The *Believer's Bible Commentary* provides a very clear explanation of what this scripture means when it says we should pray without losing heart:

> The parable of the praying widow teaches that we always ought to pray and not lose heart. This is true in a general sense of all people, and of all kinds of prayer, but the special sense in which it is used here is prayer for God's deliverance in times of testing. It is praying without losing heart during the long, weary interval between Christ's first and second comings.[32]

We are always searching for the missing piece of the puzzle in our lives because we are separated from our true source, which is God. When we are separated from our source, we often experience shame, doubt, insecurity, and loneliness, just like Adam and Eve when they disobeyed God in the garden of Eden—they were instantly disconnected from their source. They experienced emotions new to them, and suddenly they knew what insecurity and rejection was all about, and so they hid themselves from God.

> And the LORD called unto Adam, and said unto him, where art thou? And he said, I heard thy voice in the garden, and I was afraid, because I was naked; and I hid myself. And he said, who told thee that thou wast naked? Hast thou eaten of the tree, whereof I commanded thee that thou shouldest not eat?
>
> Genesis 3:9–11, KJV

Satan wants us to believe in the power of our own independence and to think that we can solve our problems separate from God. He wants us to be just like Adam and Eve, striving to live as we want to. Satan wants us to rely on ourselves, our education, our jobs, our spouses, and our parents as a way of handling life's difficulties. But unless we make God our daily place of refuge, we will lack the angelic protection promised to us in Psalm 91:

> He that dwelleth in the secret place of the Most High shall abide under the shadow of the

Almighty. I will say of the LORD, He is my refuge and my fortress: my God; in him will I trust. Surely he shall deliver thee from the snare of the fowler, and from the noisome pestilence. He shall cover thee with his feathers, and under his wings shalt thou trust: his truth shall be thy shield and buckler. Thou shalt not be afraid for the terror by night; nor for the arrow that flieth by day; Nor for the pestilence that walketh at darkness; nor for the destruction that wasteth at noonday. A thousand shall fall at thy side, and ten thousand at thy right hand; but it shall not come nigh thee. Only with thine eyes shalt thou behold and see the reward of the wicked. Because thou hast made the LORD, which is my refuge, even the Most High, thy habitation; There shall no evil befall thee, neither shall any plague come nigh thy dwelling. For he shall give his angels charge over thee, to keep thee in all thy ways. They shall bear thee up in their hands, lest thou dash thy foot against a stone. Thou shall tread upon the lion and adder; the young lion and the dragon shalt thou trample under feet

Psalm 91:1–14, KJV

Our persecution can bring much glory to God when afterwards we are resurrected in the workplace. However, we must understand that when we hurt another person, we are hurting God, because everyone is a God-made creature and we are all tied to the blood of Adam and Eve.

Seeking a promotion in the workplace to fill a void

in your life is like building your kingdom in the sand—sooner or later the wind comes along and blows your little kingdom away, and with the passing of time you are not remembered because you planted your garden in the sand. I am reminded of a story that was sent to me by a dear friend while I was writing this chapter. This story parallels the point I am making about a quickly built sand kingdom:

This is a story about two friends who were walking through a desert.

At one point the two got into an argument and one friend hit the other in the face.

The one who was hit was hurt, but instead of retaliating he simply bent down and wrote these words in the sand: *Today my best friend hit me in my face.*

They walked on until they found an oasis where they decided to cool off in the water.

The one who had been hit got stuck in the mud and was drowning, but the friend saved him. When the drowning man came to, he found a large rock and carved these words into it: *Today my best friend saved my life.*

The friend who had hit him and then saved him asked, "After I hit you, you wrote it in the sand, but when I saved your life, you carved it into stone. Why did you do this?"

The man answered, "When someone hurts us we must write it in the sand where the wind of forgiveness can blow it away. But if someone does a good deed for us, we must carve it into stone where the wind can't blow it away. Learn to write the hurt in the sand and carve your good experiences in stone."

—Author Unknown

Rewards in the workplace cannot always be about money. One of the strongest statements you can make in a workplace setting as a Christian woman is to let other women know you value them and their work.

Henry Kaiser once said that "you would automatically practice good human relations if you would remember that every individual is important, because every individual is a child of God."

A woman who is satisfied with herself will be satisfied with others. Just like in a marriage relationship, a man and woman can only satisfy each other if they are satisfied in themselves. In other words, if you want to get treated like a queen, you must select a man who is connected to the true King (God).

A Prayer for Wednesday in the Workplace

Good Morning, Jesus! I slow myself down for a moment so that I may sense your presence. Today is Wednesday, and I welcome you into my workplace to allow your spirit to rest on me until I can execute all tasks without mistakes.

Wednesday is my favorite day of the week, not because it is "over-the-hump day," but because it is a time to look back, to take stock, and to reflect on my attitude over the past two days to determine whether it was good or bad. It is time for careful thoughts and prayers of thanksgiving.

Help me at the end of each weary and demanding day to go up into the mountain like Jesus did for a few moments of reflection and prayer in the presence of the Father.

Dear Lord, help me to make the best use of my time throughout the remainder of the work-week as I work, serve, and live to honor you.

As this day winds to a close, help me find a way to get alone to pray the Lord's Prayer:

"Our Father, which art in heaven, hallowed be Thy name. Thy Kingdom come. Thy will be done in earth, as it is in heaven. Give us this day our daily bread. And forgive us our debts, as we forgive our debtors. Lead us not into temptation, but deliver us from evil; for thine is the kingdom, and the power, and the glory, for ever. Amen" (KJV).

Remind me of the admonition of your Word in Matthew 6:14–15 where Jesus said, "For if ye forgive men their trespasses, your heavenly father will also forgive you: But if ye forgive not men their trespasses, neither will your father forgive your trespasses" (KJV).

As I close my prayer, Holy Spirit, please reside in me. I'm depending on you to see me through this workday. You know my needs and my desires. Lead and direct me into everything that is good and perfect. Strengthen me to accomplish every task that is assigned to me today in the workplace. Help me not to faint when challenges arrive. Help me to recall your words so that I am able to work to the glory of God and not man.

In Jesus' name I pray, amen!

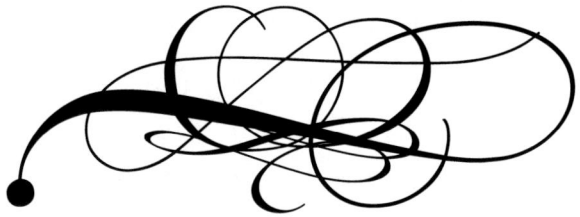

Chapter 5
God's Etiquette for Hurting Women in the Workplace

Barbara is a successful Christian woman who has more than seventeen years of experience in the corporate world. However, she did not graduate from college. Although her behavior is polished, you would not know that she is a hurting woman until you have an opportunity to work closely with her. Barbara's insecurity is displayed through her desire to control and give out misleading information to maintain the persona that she is the most knowledgeable person in the office. Barbara has gone through a bitter divorce and masks her pain by being an overachiever in the workplace. Barbara is an older woman and feels that she should be farther up the ladder in her career after seventeen years. She is wearied waiting for God's promotion. So to hurry God along, Barbara has devised her only immoral scheme to get ahead. When Barbara was finally promoted to a supervisor position, it was eliminated three months later due to the downsizing of the organization. Barbara now has an entry-level position and is starting all over again in a new industry. What is saddest about Barbara is that she really does love God, but she is still a hurting woman. Her lip testimony is different from her behavioral testimony because she is not using God's etiquette in the workplace.

> Treat people as if they were what they ought to be and you help them to become what they are capable of being.
>
> —Johann Wolfgang Von Goethe

So often it is hard to separate the hurting, unsaved women in the workplace from the healed Christian women in the workplace. This is not to say that as Christian women we will not have problems, but our attitudes should be adjusted. "Many are the afflictions of the righteous; but the LORD delivereth him out of them all" (Psalm 34:19, KJV). Many women of God get impregnated with the Word on Sunday but then have a miscarriage on Monday. This normally happens because many women confuse church attendance with having a relationship with God. Church becomes a substitute for reading and studying the Bible independently. Therefore, when they enter the workplace on Monday, Satan is already prepared to abort everything that was planted in them on Sunday.

> Many women of God are impregnated with the Word on Sunday but have a miscarriage on Monday.

> These people come near to me with their mouth and honor me with their lips, but their hearts are far from me. Their worship of me is made up only of rules taught by men says the LORD.
>
> Isaiah 29:13, NIV

Hurting women often have the same academic knowledge and skills as those who've been healed, but their social relationships suffer; often they have not matured out of their pain, and so they function like a child instead of like a responsible adult. They are stuck in a prison of their own making today because they are still living with yesterday's pain. Unresolved pain and guilt can cause the ghosts of our past to walk the halls of our minds and hearts. In order to rid "the haunted house" of our souls from these ghosts, we must forgive and forget.

> Unresolved pain and guilt can cause the ghosts of our past to walk the halls of our minds and hearts.

As Christian women, we should realize that the workplace is the only place where non-Christian women get the chance to find out what God is like, and they do so by watching our godly behavior. But sadly, most of the time the God they see displayed through us makes them want to have nothing to do with our confessed faith. We should remember that as Christians we are always being "interviewed"—whether in a relaxed or a formal setting. Non-Christian women are watching what we preach in our actions and behavior toward others. We should avoid behavior that could be perceived as disrespectful, discourteous, or abrasive. We should always remember to be courteous and thoughtful to people around us, regardless of what may be going on in our lives. By having servants' hearts, we realize that our hurt does not have to consume us, because we can forge ahead through our pain by helping someone else find healing.

Impressing our boss with empty promises and arrogant speech isn't enough in the corporate world, and the same applies to our heavenly boss. He is more interested in how well we build relationships with our peers and subordinates than he is with the empty fanfare of mere words.

In order to make a good impression during an interview, we must follow the guidelines outlined by our supreme boss, the Creator of heaven and earth. These guidelines also define the godly etiquette that we should display in the workplace:

1. Arrive to work on time with a song in your mind and the Word in your heart.

> "Speaking to yourselves in psalms and hymns and spiritual songs, singing and making melody in your heart to the LORD; Giving thanks always for all things unto God and the father in the name of our LORD Jesus Christ" (Ephesians 5:19–20, KJV).

2. Work every day as if you are working for the Lord, and avoid gossiping.

> "Whatever you do, do it heartily, as working for the LORD, not unto men" (Colossians 3:23 KJV).

> "That ye put off concerning the former conversation, the old man, which is corrupt according to the deceitful lusts; and be renewed in the spirit of your mind; And that ye put on the new man, which after God is created in righteousness and true holiness" (Ephesians 4:22–24, KJV).

3. Always behave in a friendly manner to your co-workers.

> "God offers his friendship to the godly" (Proverbs 3:32, NLT).

> "Why do you criticize and pass judgment on your brother? Or you, why do you look down upon or despise your brother? For we shall all stand before the judgment seat of God. For it is written, As I live, says the LORD, every knee shall bow to Me, and every tongue shall confess to God. And so each of us shall give an account of himself to God" (Romans 14:10–12, TAB).

4. Be service-minded toward others in the workplace and show empathy at all times.

> "Then let us no more criticize and blame and pass judgment on one another, but rather decide and endeavor never to put a stumbling block or an obstacle or a hindrance in the way of a brother" (Romans 14:13, TAB).

5. Put your co-workers and customers first, and strive to encourage others even when the results have yet to appear.

> "Let nothing be done through strife or vainglory; but in lowliness of mind let each esteem other better than themselves. Look not every man on his own things, but every man also on the things of others" (Philippians 2:3–4, KJV).

6. Let co-workers' needs take precedence over serving your own needs.

"And He said to all, If any person wills to come after Me, let him deny himself (disown himself, forget, lose sight of himself and his own interests, refuse and give up himself) and take up his cross daily and follow Me (cleave steadfastly to Me, conform wholly to My example in living and, if need be, in dying also). For whoever, would preserve his life and save it will lose and destroy it, but whoever loses his life for my sake, he will preserve and save it (from the penalty of external death) for what does it profit a man, if he gains the whole world and ruins or forfeits (loses) himself?" (Luke 9:23–25, TAB).

"Greater love hath no man than this, that a man lay down his life for his friends. Ye are my friends, if ye do whatsoever I command you" (John 15:13–14, KJV).

7. Have a vision of yourself in the workplace that is positive and that can be replicated by others.

> "Where there is no vision (no redemptive revelation of God), the people perish; but he who keeps the law (of God, which includes that of man) blessed (happy, fortunate, and enviable) is he" (Proverbs 29:18, TAB).

8. Be a source of inspiration to others in the workplace.

> "You are the light of the world. A city set on a hill cannot be hidden. Nor do men light a lamp and put it under a peck measure, but on a lampstand, and it gives light to all in the house. Let your

light so shine before men that they may see your moral excellence and your praiseworthy, noble, and good deeds and recognize and honor and praise and glorify your Father who is in heaven" (Matthew 5:14–16, TAB).

9. Say what you mean and mean what you say when you are dealing with others in the workplace.

   "He who guards his mouth and his tongue keeps himself from troubles" (Proverbs 21:23, TAB).

10. Show humility toward co-workers and customers.

    "Therefore humble yourselves (demote, lower yourselves in your own estimation) under the mighty hand of God, that in due time He may exalt you" (1 Peter 5:6, TAB).

11. Strive to facilitate good working relationships and enhanced efficiency.

    "Let no foul or polluting language, nor evil word nor unwholesome or worthless talk (ever) come out of your mouth, but only such (speech) as is good and beneficial to the spiritual progress of others, as is fitting to the need and the occasion, that it may be a blessing and give grace (God's favor) to those who hear it" (Ephesians 4:29, TAB).

12. Always practice impeccable grooming. Even though God is more concerned with what resides in the heart, good grooming shows respect for ourselves as well as for the professional aspect of our jobs.

"Let not yours be the (merely) external adorning with (elaborate) interweaving and knotting of the hair, the wearing of jewelry, or changes of clothes; But let it be the inward adorning and beauty of the hidden person of the heart, with the incorruptible and unfading charm of a gentle and peaceful spirit, which (is not anxious or wrought up, but) is very precious in the sight of God" (1 Peter 3:3–4, TAB).

13. Stay optimistic when things go wrong in the workplace.

"This is the day which the LORD hath made; we will rejoice and be glad in it" (Psalms 118:24, KJV).

14. Stay motivated by meeting God's standard of excellence in the workplace.

"Being confident of this very thing, that he which hath begun a good work in you will perform it until the day of Christ Jesus" (Philippians 1:6, KJV).

15. Complete all tasks in a timely manner; always walk in integrity and strive for excellence.

"Then this Daniel was distinguished about the presidents and the satraps because an excellent spirit was in him, and the king thought to set him over the whole realm" (Daniel 6:3, TAB).

16. Do not grumble, complain, or find fault with co-workers.

"Do all things without grumbling and faultfinding and complaining (against God) and questioning and doubting (among yourselves), That you may show yourselves to be blameless and guileless, innocent and uncontaminated, children of God without blemish (faultless, unrebukable) in the midst of a crooked and wicked generation, among whom you are seen as bright lights (stars or beacons shining our clearly) in the (dark) world" (Philippians 2:14–15, TAB).

17. Be a good listener, and when it's your turn to speak, be thoughtful and considerate.

    "Wherefore, my beloved brethren, let every man be swift to hear, slow to speak, slow to wrath: For the wrath of man worketh not the righteousness of God" (James 1:19–20, KJV).

18. Guard your heart in the workplace and be wise when sharing intimate details with co-workers because privacy is a virtue.

    "I wisdom dwell with prudence" (Proverbs 8:12, KJV).

A Prayer for Thursday in the Workplace

Good Morning, Jesus! I slow myself down
for a moment so that I may sense your presence.
Today is Thursday, and I welcome you into my
workplace to allow your spirit to rest on me until
I can execute all tasks without mistakes.

Oh gracious Jesus, I have need of patience and endurance to make it to the end of the workweek. As your
Word tells us in Hebrews 10:36, "We have need of
steadfast patience and endurance, so that we may perform and fully accomplish the will of God, and thus
receive and carry away what is promised" (TAB).

Let me not experience stagnation or sell out for self-
gratification over true work transformation. I ask
today that You not change my boss, my co-workers, the cleaning crew, or the president of the company, but I ask that today you would change me.

Whatever happens today in the workplace, please don't
leave me, heavenly Father. Don't let unexpected circumstances and problems change me either. Don't let
me be afraid today, don't let me get angry, don't let me
get impatient, but instead … make me just like you.

Help me to work diligently until the workweek is over,
so that like Paul I may "press on to take hold of that
for which Christ Jesus took hold of me. Brothers, I do
not consider myself yet to have taken hold of it. But

one thing I do: forgetting what is behind and straining toward what is ahead, I press on toward the goal to win the prize for which God has called me heavenward in Christ Jesus" (Philippians 3:12–14, TAB).

As I close my prayer, Holy Spirit, please reside in me. I'm depending on you to see me through this workday. You know my needs and my desires. Lead and direct me into everything that is good and perfect. Strengthen me to accomplish every task that is assigned to me today in the workplace. Help me not to faint when challenges arrive. Help me to recall your words so that I may work to the glory of God and not man.

In Jesus' name I pray, amen!

Chapter 6
Strategies for Helping a Hurting Woman in the Workplace

Angie is a successful professional nurse who is sometimes compared to a saint in her workplace. Some co-workers mistake Angie for being a nun because of her noble ways and desire to help the poor and needy. Angie has been a nurse with Heaven Healthcare facility for more than fifteen years and has been promoted several times. Even with all of her promotions, Angie wants to go higher and higher in her workplace. Angie is being robbed by Satan in having true contentment because she still feels like a failure. Angie grew up in a middle-class family and attended an all-girls college. She is married to a wonderful husband and has three beautiful children. Yet with all of these accomplishments, Angie has a longing in her heart that she feels will only be filled by obtaining more external power. Angie has a wounded heart before the Lord. Angie is so defined by external roles (mom, wife, daughter, nurse, supervisor, sister, and other roles) that she has forgotten to sit in the presence of Jesus. Angie does not realize that her soul is simply starving to sit in Jesus' presence like Mary, so she runs around in the workplace with Martha's mentality that busyness will equal to contentment, peace, and joy. Angie, like so many other women, has planted her heart in the workplace, and she no longer hears her own authentic music playing within her divine soul.

> But those who wait for the LORD (who expect, look for, and hope in Him) shall change and renew their strength and power; they shall lift their wings and mount up (close to God) as eagles (mount up to the sun); they shall run and not be weary, they shall walk and not faint or become tired.
>
> Isaiah 40:31, TAB

God sees all of our past mistakes and our past hurts, and he knows all about our future. God keeps a close watch on all of his creation, and he knows when even one suffers. I find this very comforting, especially when everything else in the world is so full of uncertainty. We have this assurance that God is always just a prayer away.

An important aspect of helping a hurting woman heal God's way is to get them to come to grips with their internal pain. They must face the fact that dulling their pain by drowning in their sorrows in the workplace is only a temporary fix. It is impossible to walk on our God-ordained spiritual path when we are immobilized by fear and pain. To arrive at a place of serenity, we must carry our own baggage in order to be healed.

If you are a hurting woman in the workplace, it probably feels like the pain inside of you is swelling like huge ocean waves in the midst of a storm, and it seems impossible to hear the still, small voice of Jesus in the midst of the howling winds. It is only after the storm has ceased that you can hear the message being thrust onto the shores by the waves. If you take a walk on that shore after the storm, you will find answers in the broken pieces of debris scattered everywhere. When you look back at the now-calm ocean and remember your terrible ordeal, you triumphantly realize that you are the victor, not the victim.

I am thankful that flowing from my heart is love and gratitude. I am grateful that I can now tell my story and share my hurt because I have surrendered all to God. As hurting women we must first give our lives to Jesus Christ. Then, as Christian women we must remember and recognize that all of us have a cross to bear if we want to be a follower of Jesus Christ. Mark 8:34 (TAB) states, "If anyone intends to come after me, let him deny himself (forget, ignore, disown, and lose insight of himself and his own interests) and take up his cross, and (joining Me as a disciple and siding with My Party) follow with Me (continually, cleaving steadfastly to Me)."

There are going to be times in your life even as a Christian when you will experience pain, disappointments, and setbacks; however, as you go through these difficult circumstances, you must stay focused on Jesus and not let fear drive your life.

Your pain is your training ground for becoming a heavyweight champion in the kingdom of God. With God as your spiritual fitness trainer, you've got to go through some things. You've got to get up every morning and get a thirty-minute workout in the Word. You've got to cross-train in the discipline of praying morning, noon, and evening; and you've got to lift weights through fasting and meditating on his Word.

> Your pain is your training ground for becoming a heavyweight champion in the Kingdom of God. With God as your spiritual fitness trainer, you've got to go through some things. You've got to get up every morning and get a thirty-minute workout in the Word. You've got to cross-train in the discipline of praying morning, noon, and evening, and you've got to lift weights through fasting and meditating on his Word.

To get over the hurt, we must be willing to keep walking on this road to Calvary. And as a walker to Calvary you must be more than just a churchgoer; you must also be a disciple. A disciple is committed to the journey and will not let a setback throw them back to the past. As a disciple, you are going to have to encounter some things and walk the same path of Jesus where, at times, you may feel forsaken. But if you hang in there you will have an amazing testimony: "I came through that ordeal and it did not destroy me."

Hurting women in the workplace struggle because their focus is on the problem and not the problem-solver—almighty God. Hurting women in the workplace must begin to learn that the only way to be free from the bondage of pain is to lean on Jesus.

> Now the LORD is that Spirit: and where the Spirit of the LORD is, there is liberty.
>
> 2 Corinthians 3:17, KJV

Wherever Jesus Christ is recognized as Lord, there is freedom from the bondage of the law as well as freedom to gaze upon his face openly without anything between you and your Lord.[33]

God is our source for everything—not the jobs we hold, not the money we have in the bank, and not the house we reside in. God is our only supplier of all that is good and perfect. If you want to change your behavior in the workplace, you must look to Jesus and not other co-workers. You must keep your mind focused on his great powers and not on your troubles and pain. He knows that all of us are messed up emotionally. He won't reject us because we have faults; instead, he welcomes us into his presence for healing.

We must also remember that we are heirs of heaven, because at the cross we became blood relatives with Jesus. This inheritance is nothing we could request, work for, or deserve. It was God's legacy to the world that was being restored in Jesus' crucifixion, resurrection, and ascension back to heaven—his eternal home and ours.

Also, to overcome hurt we must realize that we can never be another woman's savior but only a vehicle through which we can introduce God's salvation. It can be exhausting acting like someone else. It is essential for you to have your own identity if you wish to recover from your past pain. No one ever made this concept clearer than John the Baptist, who was "the voice of one crying in the wilderness, 'Prepare ye the way of the Lord, make his paths straight'" (Luke 3:4, KJV). This scripture renews my spirit, because John did not try to compare himself to Jesus; instead he accepted and understood that his self-worth and value came through his connection to the Messiah.

The same is true for Jesus; he never followed the crowd. He often walked among the crowd, or the crowds followed after and found him. John 12:12–13 says, "On the next day much people that were come to the feast, when they heard that Jesus was coming to Jerusalem, took branches of palm trees, and went forth to meet him, and cried, Hosanna Blessed is the King of Israel that cometh in the name of the Lord." He was able to radically change lives because he did not run with the crowd. Jesus also was a very private person.

> And in the morning, long before daylight, He got up and went out to a deserted place, and there he prayed. And Simon (Peter) and those who were with him followed Him (pursuing Him eagerly and hunting Him out).
>
> Mark 1:35, TAB

Jesus, the Servant of Jehovah, opened his ear each morning to receive daily instructions from God the Father (Isaiah 50:4, 5). If the Lord Jesus felt the need for this early morning quiet time, how much more should we? Notice too that he prayed at a time that probably wasn't very convenient for him—he rose and went to pray long before daylight. Prayer should not be a matter of personal convenience but of self-discipline and sacrifice. Maybe our tendency to take the easy road explains why so much of our service is ineffective.[34]

Every painful experience you've encountered in your life has been orchestrated by Satan as his way of fighting with God. Therefore, your enemy is *not* the person who has caused you pain, but Satan, who delegates these individuals to inflict harm unconsciously.

> And you said in your heart, I will ascend to heaven; I will exalt my throne above the stars of God; I will sit upon the mount of assembly in the uttermost north. I will ascend above the heights of the Clouds; I will make myself like the Most High.
>
> Isaiah 14:13–14, TAB

It is always easier to cope with a difficult situation by blaming others. This response to problems was used even at the beginning of time when Adam and Eve fell from grace. When God confronted Eve, she said, "The serpent deceived me, and I ate" (Genesis 3:13), and Adam said, "The woman thou gavest me to be with, she gave me from the tree, and I ate" (Genesis 3:12, KJV).

Blaming others also creates an alibi that prevents the hurting person from truly healing. God will judge us for both our good and bad deeds in the workplace, because our job is also (or should be) a place of ministry.

> Therefore, whether we are at home (on earth away from him) or away from home (and with Him), we are constantly ambitious and strive earnestly to be pleasing to Him. For we must all appear and be revealed as we are before the judgement seat of Christ, so that each one may receive (his pay) according to what he has done in the body, whether good or evil.
>
> 2 Corinthians 5:9–10, TAB

The believer should make it his aim to be well-pleasing to the Lord. While his salvation is not dependent on works, his reward in a coming day will be directly proportionate to his faithfulness to the Lord. A believer should always remember that faith is linked with salvation, and works are linked with reward. He is saved by grace through faith, not of works; but once he is saved, he should be ambitious to perform good works, and far so doing he will receive rewards.[35]

The Bible in these verses is making it clear that each of us must give an account for our behavior on this earth. We will not be able to use our childhood, our past hurts, unloving parents, unsaved co-workers, and false preachers as an alibi as to why we did not live victoriously at all times by avoiding sin.

Here are some strategies that are scripturally based to help you begin to heal God's way:

1. Admit that you are hurting, and then surrender your pain to God.

    "Thou wilt keep him in perfect peace, whose mind is stayed on thee; because he trusteth in thee" (Isaiah 26:3, KJV).

2. Identify the source of your pain and any unresolved issues from the past.

    "Do not fret or have any anxiety about anything, but in every circumstance and in everything, by prayer and petition (definite requests), with thanksgiving, continue to make your wants known to God" (Philippians 4:6, TAB).

3. Choose one of these issues to work on through constant prayer and meditation, asking God to intervene and help you conquer the problem.

    "Calleth those things which be not as though they were" (Romans 4:17, KJV).

4. Ask God to show you his purpose for your life, and then begin doing one thing per day that will get you closer to his plan for your life.

    "The LORD answered me and said, write the vision, and make it plain upon tablets, that he may run that readeth it. For the vision is yet for an appointed time; but at the end it shall speak, and not lie: though it tarry wait for it; because it will surely come, it will not tarry" (Habakkuk 2:2, KJV).

5. Ask God to give you a sense of humor in the workplace.

    "Only be sure as citizens so to conduct yourselves (that) your manner of life (will be) worthy of the good news (the gospel) of Christ, so that whether I (do) come and see you or am absent, I may hear this of you: that you are standing firm in united spirit and purpose, striving side by side and contending with a single mind for the faith of the glad tidings (the gospel)" (Philippians 1:27, TAB).

6. Keep inspirational thoughts, poems, prayers, and books at your desk that you can read on your lunch break instead of gossiping with co-workers.

"Cause me to hear your loving-kindness in the morning, for on you do I lean and in you do I trust. Cause me to know the way wherein I should walk, for I lift up my inner self to you" (Psalms 143:8, TAB).

7. Write encouraging notes to other co-workers. Sometimes by serving others we realize our problems are minor compared to what they're facing.

> "And he said unto me, My grace is sufficient for thee: for my strength is made perfect in weakness. Most gladly therefore will I rather glory in my infirmities, that the power of Christ may rest upon me. Therefore I take pleasure in infirmities, in reproaches, in necessities, in persecutions, in distresses for Christ's sake: for when I am weak, then am I strong" (2 Corinthians 12:9–10, KJV).

8. Forgive yourself and the ones who wronged you, and then move own, because revenge is a heavy load to carry.

> "Let all bitterness and indignation and wrath and resentment and quarreling and slander be banished from you, with all malice. And become useful and helpful and kind to one another, tenderhearted, forgiving one another, as God in Christ forgave you" (Ephesians 4:31–32, TAB).

9. Be willing to give co-workers a second chance.

> "For by the grace (unmerited favor of God) given to me I warn everyone among you not to estimate

and think of himself more highly than he ought (not to have an exaggerated opinion of his own importance), but to rate his ability with sober judgment, each according to the degree of faith apportioned by God to him" (Romans 12:3, TAB).

10. Make peace with your past and then release it to God.

   "I spread forth my hands to you; my soul thirsts after You like a thirsty land (for water)" (Psalm 143:6, TAB).

11. Love your enemies and pray for those co-workers who persecute you without cause.

   "Be ye angry, and sin not: let not the sun go down upon your wrath: Neither give place to the devil" (Ephesians 4:26–27, KJV).

12. Look at the good qualities of co-workers and ignore negative behavior and comments.

   "The spirit of the LORD will come upon you in power and you will be changed into a different person" (1 Samuel 10:6, KJV).

13. Stop judging others and practice having a non-judgmental attitude; this will cause understanding, compassion, and acceptance to flow into your life.

   "Be not deceived; God is not mocked; for whatsoever a man soweth, that shall he also reap. For he that soweth to his flesh shall of the flesh reap corruption; but he that soweth to the Spirit shall of the Spirit reap life everlasting. And let us not be weary in well doing: for in due season we shall reap, if we faint not" (Galatians 6:7–9, KJV).

14. Practice unconditional love by reaching out to hurting women who may be showing intense, ugly emotions toward you such as anger, bitterness, and sarcasm.

   "Therefore encourage (admonish, exhort) one another and edify (strengthen and build up) one another, just as you are doing" (1 Thessalonians 5:11, TAB).

15. Let the hurting person find a safe place in you to share their feelings, and do not judge their pain or merely put a band-aid over it.

   "For all have sinned, and come short of the glory of God" (Romans 3:23, KJV).

16. Be willing to share your own times of struggle as well as the painful experiences of your life.

   "And not only so, but we glory in tribulations also: knowing that tribulation worketh patience; and patience, experience; and experience hope: And hope maketh not ashamed; because the love of God is shed abroad in our hearts by the Holy Ghost which is given unto you" (Romans 5:3–5, KJV).

   "All we like sheep have gone astray, we have turned every one to his own way" (Isaiah 53:6, TAB).

17. Put love in action in the workplace by showing compassion toward co-workers.

   "Owe no man any thing, but to love one another:

for he that loveth another hath fulfilled the law"
(Proverbs 17:27, KJV).

18. Let a calm spirit reside in you in the workplace.

   "He who has knowledge spares his words, and a
   man of understanding is of a calm spirit" (Proverbs 17:27).

A Prayer for Friday in the Workplace

Good Morning, Jesus! I slow myself down for a moment so that I may sense your presence. Today is Friday, and I welcome you into my workplace to allow your spirit to rest on me until I can execute all tasks without mistakes.

Thank you, Jesus, that I made it through another work-week as a vessel through which you were able to work. Thank you that the work I performed this week was the only picture of you the unbelievers were able to see.

Thank you for those things that went wrong this week and for the things that went right. Thank you for helping me let nothing discourage me, because all things work together for the good for those who love the Lord.

Thank you for this eternal truth—that if we confess our sins, you are faithful and just to forgive us and cleanse us from all unrighteousness. Lord, you are the light of my salvation; who shall I fear? You are the strength of my life; in whom shall I be afraid? Lord, you said one can chase a thousand, but two (you and me) can put ten thousand to flight.

As I close my prayer, Holy Spirit, please reside in me. I'm depending on you to see me through this workday. You know my needs and my desires. Lead and direct me into everything that is good and perfect. Strengthen me to accomplish every task that is assigned to me today in the workplace. Help me not to faint when challenges arrive. Help me to recall your words, so that I may work to the glory of God and not man.

In Jesus' name I pray, amen!

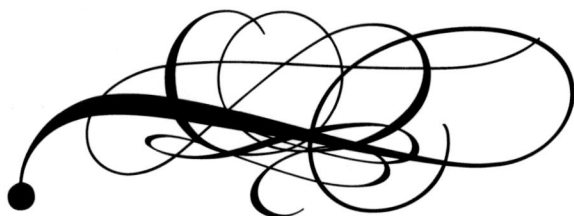

Chapter 7
Conclusions

Martha's resilience and persistence in the workplace has earned her the title of a virtuous woman. Martha, even as the vice president of the largest health care industry in her town, has always viewed the women she worked with as an opportunity to fellowship with the brokenhearted. Martha shared her life experiences with any and everyone who would listen in the workplace without feeling ashamed and doubtful because she is a healed woman of God.

Martha endured very cruel treatment at the hands of her father. Martha was physically and emotionally abused. Martha used her faith to help her deal with the ordeal. Martha's relief came from knowing that there was value in her abuse because God had a plan for her life to help other hurting women. Martha shifted her focus to her all-sustaining God and, as result, became a resilient woman instead of a brokenhearted woman. Thank God for women like Martha in the workplace who have gone through many challenges and trials but have endured them all through unwavering faith and/or left to tell how they survived.

Martha's résumé with God is long, but it gives us a refreshing renewal that God will walk with you in the work-

place. Her longstanding relationship with God as a virtuous woman has helped so many other women in the workplace find the path to walking in high calling. I thank the Lord for Martha, that even though everything may not always be well in her life, she is secure in the Lord. She has embraced her hard times but has kept a soft spot in her heart for other women.

> A capable, intelligent, and virtuous woman— who is he who can find her? She is far more precious than jewels and her value is far above rubies or pearls.
>
> Proverbs 31:10, TAB

The term "virtuous" means of noble character. I have chosen to close this book by talking about and acknowledging the virtuous women I have met over the past twenty years in the workplace; women who were centered, calm, loving, caring, smart, sassy, strong, vulnerable, capable, beautiful, orderly, and peaceful. They presented an image in the workplace that drew women to their office desk not just to borrow paper clips, but to receive precious words of wisdom and to find a peaceful sanctuary for their troubled minds.

> Strength and dignity are her clothing and her position is strong and secure; she rejoices over the future (the latter day or time to come, knowing that she and her family are in readiness for it)! She opens her mouth in skillful and godly Wisdom, and on her tongue is the law of kindness (giving counsel and instruction). She looks

well to how things go in her household, and the bread of idleness (gossip, discontent, and self-pity) she will not eat.

Proverbs 31:25–27, TAB

In discussing the above scripture verses, the *Believer's Bible Commentary* perfectly describes virtuous women just like some of the women I have had the privilege of meeting in the workplace.

> Clothed with industry and dignity, she faces the future with confidence. The instruction she gives to her family is a balance of wisdom and kindness. She keeps in close touch with the affairs of her household, and she does not waste time or engage in shallow, unproductive activity.[36]

To surface as a true virtuous woman in the workplace, you must live through a metaphor, where you go from being a baby girl in pink, to a child with curiosities and fears, to a student in the classroom of life, and finally to a woman who has been tested, tried, and pushed into her destiny at her own expense and pain.

> To surface as a true virtuous woman in the workplace, you must live through a metaphor, where you go from being a baby girl in pink, to a child with curiosities and fears, to a student in the classroom of life, and finally to a woman who has been tested, tried, and pushed into her destiny at her own expense and pain.

The women I met in the workplace who were spiritually and emotionally balanced were able to show God's love by following the example of Jesus when he washed his disciples' feet.

> So when He had finished washing their feet and had put on his garments and had sat down again, He said to them, "Do you understand what I have done to you?" You call Me the Teacher (master) and the LORD, and you are right in doing so, for that is what I am. If I then, your LORD and Teacher, have washed your feet, you ought to wash one another's feet. For I have given you this as an example, so that you should do (in your turn) what I have done to you.
>
> John 13:12–15, TAB

It would seem that Christ washed the feet of all the disciples. Then he put on his outer garments and sat down again to explain to them the spiritual meaning of what he had done. He opened the conversation by asking a question. The questions of the Savior make an interesting study. They form one of his most effective methods of teaching. The disciples had acknowledged Jesus to be their Teacher and Lord, and they were right in doing so. But his example showed that the highest rank in the power structure of the kingdom is that of servant. If the Lord and Teacher had washed the disciples' feet, what excuse could they have for not washing one another's feet? He was telling them that they should keep each other clean by constant fellowship over the Word. If one sees his brother growing cold or worldly, he should lovingly exhort him from the Bible.[37]

Those exquisite women that I met in the workplace were my role models and mentors who offered constant fellowship. They showed me how to behave and how not to behave. Those phenomenal women took me under their wings until I could echo, "I can do all things through Christ Jesus who strengthens me!" They kept me from growing cold and materialistic.

> Do not be deceived, God is not mocked; for whatsoever a man soweth, that shall he also reap. For he that soweth to his flesh shall of the flesh reap corruption, but he that soweth to the spirit will of the spirit reap everlasting life.
>
> Galatians 6:7–8, KJV

We reap what we sow, and we reap in greater quantities than we've sown—whether for good or for bad. In these two verses, the warning about sowing and reaping follows an exhortation on Christian giving. Viewed in that light, we see that sowing to the flesh means spending one's money on oneself—one's own pleasures and comforts. Sowing to the Spirit is using one's money for the furtherance of God's kingdom.[38]

The virtuous women friends I've come to know over the years in the workplace often ministered to their own souls while still showing mercy and peace toward their younger co-workers who were coming up through the ranks. A lot of the strong, virtuous women I encountered were raising themselves while raising us younger women. They looked into our eyes and saw their first love, their first heartbreak, their first shame, their first dream, and their first vision, and then they passed to us the baton, completing the circle of life that encompasses womanhood.

> They looked into our eyes and saw their first love, their first heartbreak, their first shame, their first dream, and their first vision, and then they passed to us the baton, completing the circle of life that encompasses womanhood.

These virtuous women were capable of uplifting, educating, and inspiring. They would never be caught fraternizing, criticizing, destroying, and gossiping with other women. In addition, they demanded and declared that God would look beyond our faults and see our needs. They guided, healed, and directed us to our rightful paths in the workplace.

> He who is greatest among you shall be your servant. Whoever exalts himself (with haughtiness and empty pride) shall be humbled (brought low), and whoever humbles himself (whoever has a modest opinion of himself and behave accordingly) shall be raised to honor.
>
> Matthew 23:11–12, TAB

Once again the revolutionary character of the kingdom of heaven is seen in the fact that true greatness is exactly opposite to what people suppose. Jesus said, "He who is greatest among you shall be your servant. And whoever exalts himself will be humbled, and he who humbles himself will be exalted." True greatness stoops to serve.[39]

These virtuous women took care of us and stooped down and served us in the workplace. They allowed us to ask questions and to release our fears and tears without ever judging our past mistakes or actions. They could be trusted with our deepest dreams, our secret desires, our intimate ideas, and our thoughts. These virtuous women would never convey our aspirations and dreams to another breathing soul without our permission.

They planted seeds of hope, encouragement, and restoration. They uprooted all manner of evil weeds that would've spread negativity, shame, doubt, and confusion in the workplace. They sang praises to God and thanked him for every woman they were able to nurture back to emotional health, renewing that woman's strength and restoring her purpose.

> "It is because of the LORD's mercy and loving-kindness that we are not consumed, because His (tender) compassions fail not"
>
> Lamentations 3:22, TAB

With a prayer to God to remember his bitter plight, yet with lingering depression over his misery, the prophet gets his eyes off himself and onto the Lord. Hope is revived when he remembers that the Lord's mercies and compassions ... are new every morning, and that His faithfulness is great.[40]

These "unforgettable" women will never be forgotten because they played such a significant role in the workplace by walking in the life God had predestined for them. These women were wide-awake and alert, not sleepwalking through life. They had decided to be the women God created them to be, without limitations and without regrets.

Virtuous women who have recovered from their pain have a level of joy that is different from just being happy. Joy is "an intense and ecstatic or exultant happiness or the expression or manifestation of such feeling."[41] The women who embraced me taught me how to find internal joy, even when being hated by others. To preserve your joy in the midst of fiery trials you must always remember that "weeping may endure for a night, but joy comes in the morning" (Psalm 30:5, KJV). Joy can only be found in the presence of God.

> In your presence is fullness of joy, at your right hand there are pleasures forevermore.
>
> Psalm 16:11, TAB

Even though Psalm 16 was written by David, the words are prophetic of what would one day be a supplication from Jesus' heart to his Father. In verse eleven, our blessed Lord has complete confidence that God will show him the path from death back to life again. This path would ultimately lead him back to heaven where he would once again be in God's presence. There he would experience fullness of joy and pleasures forevermore.[42]

If we are to truly overcome our past hurts and grow into self-sufficient and independent Christian women, we must believe unquestioningly that God loves us. He loved us so much that he gave his life for us, and anyone who calls on his name will be saved.

> Christ loved us and gave Himself up for us, a slain offering and sacrifice to God a sweet fragrance.
>
> Ephesians 5:2, TAB

Another way in which we should resemble the Lord is by walking in love. The rest of the verse explains that to walk in love means to give ourselves for others. His gift is described as an offering and a sacrifice to God. An offering is anything given to God; a sacrifice here includes the additional element of death. He was the true burnt offering, the one who was completely devoted to do the will of God; even to the death of the cross. His sacrifice of unspeakable devotion is eulogized as a sweet smelling aroma.[43]

All of our inadequacies were nailed to the cross along with Jesus. He served humankind and gave his life through death so that we would do the same. We were put here on earth to serve others. Our service must be willingly offered out of a heart filled with truth and faith; otherwise, it will be nothing more than empty deeds, and not a sweet-smelling aroma rising to heaven before God's throne.

> For even the son of man came not to have service rendered to Him, but to serve, and to give His life as a ransom for (instead of) many.
>
> Mark 10:45, TAB

The virtuous women who blessed my life in the workplace were like Mary and her cousin Elizabeth. They learned how to be blessed women. A virtuous woman knows that her position in the workplace is chosen by God and that it should be a humbling experience. She recognizes that being highly favored and blessed means carrying a burden.

Many of the virtuous women I was exposed to pressed forward because they had learned how to surrender to God; also, they had learned how to live without answered prayers and blessings that were long overdue. They were able to encourage other women to embrace their talents and gifts, even though their giftedness may have caused more problems than it solved.

This is so eloquently demonstrated when you look at Mary, who was a rural girl, a laborer, unmarried, untaught—but she was blessed by God with a blessing she could not explain, let alone comprehend. But God in his wisdom and mercy gave her a virtuous woman in her workplace to confide in—her cousin Elizabeth, who, being much older than Mary, could have annulled Mary's dreams and confidence and attempted to invalidate her blessings. She had the perfect opportunity to do so when

Mary knelt before her, afraid and uncertain, but instead Elizabeth embraced Mary and told Mary of her own miraculous pregnancy at her advanced age, which made them both realize how much their destinies would forever be entwined. (Elizabeth's son was the future John the Baptist, who would go before Jesus and preach the coming of his kingdom, and who also baptized Jesus.) Oh, how wonderful it would be if we women in the workplace would share with each other the blessings and the burdens of being highly favored of God.

If we would dare to speak the truth, we would acknowledge that we are where we are today on the corporate ladder because some virtuous woman stooped down long enough that we might climb on her back and ride piggyback into the future.

The virtuous women who guided me in the workplace, as well as outside the workplace, were unapologetic about loving themselves, which is a lot different from the women whose bitterness has caused them to lose their ability to love. Virtuous women are like Ruth and Naomi: they help each other get through a lot of tough situations, seeing each other through the good times and the bad, through marriages and divorces, through deaths and births, through relocations and evictions, through prosperity and poverty, and through courtships and remarriages.

It you want a miracle in the workplace, connect with a virtuous woman, and together give praise and thanksgiving to God. The Bible teaches us that before there were miracles performed there were also moments allocated for thanksgiving and blessings. For example, before

Elisha miraculously increased the widow's oil, he blessed it and gave thanks, and before Jesus multiplied the loaves and two fish into a meal big enough to feed thousands, he blessed that food and gave thanks. We must do the same by speaking thanksgiving into our situation as it currently exists, and *then* we will see our blessings manifested (and multiplied) in the workplace.

Also, these virtuous women who cheered me on had the audacity to do so because they had truly learned how to evoke forgiveness. When you have forgiven someone for a debt, a wrong deed, or an inconsiderate action done toward you, a settlement is not required. Forgiveness is "to excuse for a fault or an offense; to pardon. To renounce anger or resentment against; to absolve from payment."[44]

> In Him we have redemption (deliverance and salvation) through His blood, the remission (forgiveness) of our offenses (shortcomings and trespasses).
>
> Ephesians 1:7, TAB

> This describes that aspect of the work of Christ by which we are freed from the bondage and guilt of sin and introduced into a life of liberty. The Lord Jesus is the Redeemer. We are the redeemed. His blood is the ransom price; nothing less would do. One of the results of redemption is the forgiveness of sins. Forgiveness is not the same as redemption; it is one of its fruits.[45]

Virtuous women focus on *whose* they are (God's), and hurting women focus on *who* they are in reference to other women, other co-workers, other moms, other Christians, and other wives. These women are living in a spiritual place that is very far apart from God. We need to be reconciled to God because ultimately we are his— he created us.

> Yet now has (Christ, the Messiah) reconciled (you to God) in the body of His flesh through death, in order to present you holy and faultless and irreproachable in His (the father's) presence.
>
> Colossians 1:22, TAB

Jesus reconciled us to God in the body of his flesh through death. It was not by his life but by his death, so that we may be presented to God as holy, and blameless, and above reproach in his sight. What marvelous grace, that ungodly sinners like us can be delivered from our past evil life and welcomed into such a realm of blessing![46]

> You are not your own, You were brought with a price (purchased with a preciousness and paid for, made His own). So, then honor God and bring glory to Him in your body.
>
> 1 Corinthians 6:19–20, TAB

Because we are not our own, it is not our place to take our bodies and use them any way we desire. Our bodies do not belong to us; they belong to the Lord. We are the Lord's both by creation and redemption. Thus, we must use our body to glorify God, the one to whom it belongs.[47]

Hurting women will continue to walk in darkness if they follow the evil one of this world, who also deceived Adam and Eve.

If you're a hurting woman, let me encourage you with this truth: If you keep walking with God, positive change will eventually happen in your life, without a shadow of doubt. Each one of us must walk our road to Calvary, and when we do so, we will also fulfill God's plan for our life, just like Jesus did. However, if we refuse to deny ourselves and take up our cross daily and follow him, we will not be worthy of him.

> To live is Christ, and to die is gain.
>
> Philippians 1:21, NIV

The book of Philippians was written by the apostle Paul, who did not live for money, fame, or pleasure. The object of his life was to love, worship, and serve the Lord Jesus. Therefore, to him, to die was to gain. This is how it should be with us as well—to die is to be with Christ and to be like him forever. It is to serve him with an unsinning heart and with feet that never stray.[48]

We must bank everything we have on Jesus Christ. We must bank our homes, our children, our jobs, our cars, our churches, and our friends; everything must be ultimately surrendered to the supreme God. We must have our own "deep in the desert" experience with the Lord in order to fully understand his awesome presence in our lives.

Virtuous women are very different in the workplace, because they are not cut from the same cookie cutter; instead, they are all molded in the image of God. Therefore, when others operate differently from us in the workplace, we must still extend them the right hand of fellowship.

> O satisfy us with Your mercy and loving-kindness in the morning (now, before we are older), that we may rejoice and be glad all our days.
>
> Psalm 90:14, TAB

The psalmist pleads with the Lord to return to his people in mercy. Will his anger burn forever? Won't he please have compassion on them and satisfy them early with his mercy that they might live out their remaining days in a measure of tranquility and happiness?[49]

When carrying our cross in the workplace we must pray in the same manner that Jesus prayed from the cross: "Father forgive them, for they know not what they do" (Luke 23:34, TAB). The grief that we suffer in the workplace is ordained by God so that our purpose can be discovered.

> It was the will of the LORD to crush him; he has put him to grief.
>
> Isaiah 53:10, TAB

Yet the Lord saw fit to bruise him, to put him to grief. When his soul has been made an offering for sin, he will see his posterity, that is, all those who believe in him, he shall prolong his days, living in the power of an endless life. All God's purposes shall be realized through him.[50]

Virtuous women are women we can fellowship with in the workplace. They have witnessed extraordinary things in their lives and are a testimony to their survival.

> What we have seen and (ourselves) heard, we are also telling you, so that you too may realize and enjoy fellowship as partners and partakers with us. And (this) fellowship that we have (which is a distinguishing mark of Christians) is with the Father and with His, son Jesus Christ (the messiah).
>
> 1 John 1:3, TAB

The apostles did not keep the good news of the kingdom of God a secret, and neither should we. They realized that fellowship is the distinguishing mark of Christians, and so they declared it freely and fully. All who receive the testimony of the apostles have fellowship with the Father, with his son Jesus Christ, and also with the apostles and all other believers.[51]

We must join the procession of the virtuous women who have gone before us and begin claiming our rightful position in the workplace by pushing, teaching, comforting, and restoring women back to that place of safety where they can have a peaceful mind like our Savior, Jesus Christ. We must join the marching band now so that the next generation of working women will be ready to walk in their destiny in the working world without having to validate their existence by destroying another person.

Each of us matters to God, and he wants us to find our God-ordained purpose while here on earth. However, many of us will never reap our harvest because we give up too soon. For many, faith without works is dead. God is waiting on you to take steps of faithfulness to fulfill the calling he has placed in your heart.

> I know your (record of) works and what you are doing. See! I have set before you a door wide open which no one is able to shut; I know that you have put little power, and yet you have kept my Word and gathered my message and have not renounced or denied My name.
>
> Revelation 3:8, TAB

Women who are walking daily in their life purpose pray for others before they pray for themselves; they pray for people they know and even those they don't know. They care about the neighbor children and not just their own; they help mend broken hearts and serve church dinners; they love their homes and are comfortable within themselves; and they could not care less what anyone else thinks about their life choices, because they know those choices are pleasing to God.

> Create in me a clean heart, O God; and renew a right spirit within me.
>
> Psalms 51:10, KJV

Looking back on his life, David realized that all his troubles had started in his mind. He had entertained evil thoughts until at last he had committed the sins relating to such thoughts. When he writes Psalm 51, he is finally asking God to create in him a clean mind. If the fountain is clean, the stream flowing from it will also be pure and clean and free of toxins, thus helping you to be steadfast in guarding against future outbreaks of sin.[52]

We have the potential to be the next generation of women who live by paying attention to each other's pains and needs, never again destroying women in the workplace with the power of our tongue. To all those virtuous women who have crossed my path, I want to affirm that I honor you with this book, and I will continue to bear fruit from the good seeds you sowed in me by being resilient, strong, and courageous.

It is time to embrace and salute such women who blessed us and encircled us—women who could nurture, heal, and show love without acting like they were giving begrudgingly of their power from a lofty throne. To those women I want to say, "You triumphed through adversities, and now we stand on the threshold of your pain as healed women!"

> If then you have been raised with Christ (to a new life, thus sharing His resurrection from the dead), aim at and seek the (rich, external treasures) that are above, where Christ is, seated at the right hand of God. And set your minds and keep them set on what is above (the higher things), not on the things that are on the earth.
>
> Colossians 3:1–2, TAB

The spiritual meaning of this scripture is that we have said good-bye to our former way of life and have entered into a new type of life—the life of the risen Lord Jesus Christ. Because we have been raised with Christ, we should seek those things that are above; we should be cultivating heavenly ways. The Christian woman should not be earthbound in her outlook. She should view things not as they appear to her natural eye but in reference to their importance to God and to eternity.[53]

When we praise God, we are the ones being blessed, anointed, renewed, restored, revived, regenerated, and replanted.

A virtuous woman will help bear your burdens. She will not violate your confidence, but she will make you accountable for your actions. Paul had this to say about accountability:

> Brethren, if a man be overtaken in a fault, ye which are spiritual, restore such a one in the spirit of meekness; considering thyself, lest thou also be tempted. Bear ye one another's burdens, and so fulfill the law of Christ. For if a man think himself be something, when he is nothing, he deceiveth himself.
>
> Galatians 6:1–3, KJV

A truly spiritual woman will never boast of her spirituality, but instead she will have the tender heart of a shepherdess, meaning she'll want to restore back to a place of wholeness the one who has hurt or offended her. She will not act in a spirit of pride or superiority but in a spirit of gentleness, remembering that she also could easily be tempted to stumble and fall.[54]

We want these kinds of women in our lives and in the workplace—the kind who know how to restore. I pray that God will bring into your life this kind of virtuous woman, the same kind of woman that Solomon wrote about in Proverbs:

> The man of many friends (a friend of all the world) will prove himself a bad friend, but there is a friend who sticks closer than a brother.
>
> Proverbs 18:24, TAB

It is better to have one true friend than a host of friends who will lead you astray. There are friends who pretend to be friends, and then there are friends who stick closer than a true sister.[55]

Our past hurts should not be the focus of our attention but rather a reminder of God's mercy and grace. When you focus on your past hurts, you live in a perpetual state of doubt, and eventually that doubt will turn into fear. The more we dwell on the hurt, the more we get discouraged, and the less faith we have in God's ability to make us victorious.

We must bring all hurtful thoughts into captivity. In other words, we must set free the good thoughts and bind up the bad thoughts.

> Casting down imaginations, and every high thing that exalteth itself against the knowledge of God,

and bringing into captivity every thought to the obedience of Christ.

2 Corinthians 10:5, KJV

All of our thoughts and speculations must be judged in the light of the teachings of the Lord Jesus Christ. Paul was not condemning human reasoning when he wrote this, but he was warning us that we must not allow our intellects to be exercised in defiance of the Lord and in disobedience to him.[56]

When we internalize the hurt instead of making it an external battle, Satan has greater control over keeping us in that hurtful state. If you have been hurt, don't just run to your co-workers for empathy and reassurance; instead, study the Word of God and let it become your arsenal against the pain.

When Jesus was being tempted by Satan in the wilderness, he did not battle with Satan in his mind; he used the Word of God to defeat him. Jesus said to him, "It is written, you shall not tempt, test thoroughly, or try exceedingly the Lord your God" (Matthew 4:5–7, TAB).

When you fill your mind with God's Word, the hurt will have no choice but to flee, just like Satan did, and then the angels will come and minister to your soul. God has gifts for all of us already wrapped under the Christmas tree, but he cannot give those gifts to us until we let go and forgive those who've hurt us.

I have relived many of those painful days and nights in the aftermath of my workplace "ground-zero" experience. However, I know that there was a reason far beyond what I can ever write in this book that was playing a hand in my life, and when I think about this awesome power it takes my breath away. There will be many nights at your own "ground zero" when you will lay your head down on your pillow and cry. You will wonder what is wrong with you, what have you done to deserve such hurt, and you will even wonder if you are lovable. But God will send somebody in the middle of your midnight "ground zero" to help you. We are called to passionately love as sisters those hurting women who will only be in our work pathway for a brief moment in our lives, regardless of their behavior toward us.

As I close this book, I feel now that I have come full circle. Just look where God is leading you! And remember, don't let a day go by without communicating with him, so that as your path opens up beautifully before you, you'll see the way and be able to walk confidently in it.

A Prayer for Saturday in the Workplace

Good Morning, Jesus! I slow myself down
for a moment so that I may sense your presence. Today is Saturday, and I welcome you into
my workplace to allow your spirit to rest on me
until I can execute all tasks without mistakes.

Lord, I magnify you today in the workplace; I exalt you
and I lift you up. You are all-knowing and powerful;
you are God all by yourself. You are the one true living God, and I thank you for being God of my life.

Lord, you said in your Word that whatsoever we ask
for, if we ask believing, then we shall receive it. You
also said that "faith cometh by hearing and hearing by
the word of God" (Romans 10:17). I receive the promise of your Word today, which says that I shall be the
head and not the tail, the lender and not the borrower.

Lord, you have known me since birth; before I was
formed you knew me. Let me walk in my preordained
destiny in the workplace today. I am your sheep; please
attend to my needs as I go throughout the workday.

Lord, I thank you that you have blessed me in Christ,
and that you have given me all the spiritual blessings and gifts in the heavens. Let me use these gifts
to be a vessel through which you can be glorified.

I have the confidence that you have heard my
prayer and that all my needs will be met today

through Christ Jesus. I will serve every man,
woman, or child who comes across my path today
as if I am working unto you and not man.

According to your Word, Lord, I know that
no weapon formed against me shall prosper, and that every tongue that rises up against
me in judgment shall be condemned.

As I close my prayer, Holy Spirit, please reside in me.
I'm depending on you to see me through this workday.
You know my needs and my desires. Lead and direct me
into everything that is good and perfect. Strengthen me
to accomplish every task that is assigned to me today in
the workplace. Help me not to faint when challenges
arrive. Help me to recall your Word and to remember
that I am to work to the glory of God and not man.

In Jesus' name I pray, amen!

The Lord Is My Pacesetter

A Version of the Twenty-third Psalm from Japan

The Lord is my pacesetter, I shall not rush;
He makes me stop for quiet intervals.
He provides me with images of still-
ness which restore my serenity.
He leads me in the way of efficiency through calmness of mind,
and his guidance is peace.
Even though I have a great many
things to accomplish each day,
I will not fret, for his presence is here.
His timelessness and his all-impor-
tance will keep me in balance.
He prepares refreshment and renewal
in the midst of my activity
by anointing my mind with his oils of tranquility.
My cup of joy overflows.
Truly harmony and effectiveness shall
be the fruits of my hours,
for I shall walk in the pace of my Lord
and dwell in his house forever.

*If this book has helped you in any way,
I would love to hear from you as to
what God has done through his
anointed Word to change your life.
Send to ella@ellawise.com*

(Endnotes)

1   MacDonald, William. Farstad, Art, Ed. *Believer's Bible Commentary.* Thomas Nelson Publishers: Nashville, Tennesse. 1985.

2   *The Believer's Bible Commentary,* pg. 798

3   *The Believer's Bible Commentary* pg. 1377

4   *The American Heritage College Dictionary (3rd Edition)*

5   *The American Heritage College Dictionary (3RD Edition)*

6   *The American Heritage College Dictionary (3rd Edition)*

7   *The Believer's Bible Commentary,* pg.1896

8   *The Believer's Bible Commentary,* pg. 1227

9   *The Believer's Bible Commentary,* pg. 2265

10 *The Believer's Bible Commentary,* pg. 2218

11 *The Believer's Bible Commentary,* pg. 1285

12 *The Believer's Bible Commentary,* pg. 1409

13 *The Believer's Bible Commentary,* pg. 1737

14 *The Believer's Bible Commentary,* pg. 1562–1563

15 *The Believer's Bible Commentary,* pg. 1371

16 *The Believer's Bible Commentary,* pg. 2265

17 *The Believer's Bible Commentary,* pg. 1555

18 *The Believer's Bible Commentary,* pg. 798

19 *The Believer's Bible Commentary,* pg. 1512

20 *The Believer's Bible Commentary,* pg. 1288–1289

21 *The Believer's Bible Commentary,* pg. 1710–1711

22 *The Believer's Bible Commentary*, pg. 1423

23 *The Believer's Bible Commentary*, pg. 1490

24 *The Believer's Bible Commentary*, pg. 852–853

25 *The Believer's Bible Commentary*, pg. 1226

26 *The Believer's Bible Commentary*, pg. 1226

27 *The Believer's Bible Commentary*, pg. 1443

28 *The Believer's Bible Commentary*, pg. 2234–2235

29 *The Believer's Bible Commentary*, pg. 1752–1753

30 *The Believer's Bible Commentary*, pg. 970–971

31 *The Believer's Bible Commentary*, pg. 832

32 *The Believer's Bible Commentary*, pg.1437

33 *The Believer's Bible Commentary*, pg. 1831

34 *The Believer's Bible Commentary*, pg. 1323

35 *The Believer's Bible Commentary*, pg. 1839

36 *The Believer's Bible Commentary*, pg. 871

37 *The Believer's Bible Commentary*, pg. 1542–1543

38 *The Believer's Bible Commentary*, pg. 1896

39 *The Believer's Bible Commentary*, pg. 1289

40 *The Believer's Bible Commentary*, pg. 1032

41 *The American Heritage Dictionary*

42 *The Believer's Bible Commentary*, pg. 568

43 *The Believer's Bible Commentary*, pg. 1941

44 *The American Heritage Dictionary*

45 *The Believer's Bible Commentary*, pg. 1909

46   *The Believer's Bible Commentary*, pg. 1996

47   *The Believer's Bible Commentary*, pg. 1764–1765

48   *The Believer's Bible Commentary*, pg. 1963

49   *The Believer's Bible Commentary*, pg. 689

50   *The Believer's Bible Commentary*, pg. 980

51   *The Believer's Bible Commentary*, pg. 2309

52   *The Believer's Bible Commentary*, pg. 630

53   *The Believer's Bible Commentary*, pg. 2007

54   *The Believer's Bible Commentary*, pg. 1895

55   *The Believer's Bible Commentary*, pg. 839

56   *The Believer's Bible Commentary*, pg. 1856